£12,80

before the
u will be

The

TKT

Teaching Knowledge Test

Course

KAL Module

Knowledge About Language

David Albery

Published in collaboration with Cambridge ESOL

UNIVERSITY *of* **CAMBRIDGE**
ESOL Examinations

English for Speakers of Other Languages

CAMBRIDGE
UNIVERSITY PRESS

CAMBRIDGE UNIVERSITY PRESS
Cambridge, New York, Melbourne, Madrid, Cape Town,
Singapore, São Paulo, Delhi, Tokyo, Mexico City

Cambridge University Press
The Edinburgh Building, Cambridge CB2 8RU, UK

www.cambridge.org
Information on this title: www.cambridge.org/9780521154369

First published 2012

Printed in the United Kingdom at the University Press, Cambridge

A catalogue record for this publication is available from the British Library

ISBN 978-0-521-15436-9 Paperback

Contents

Acknowledgements

Many thanks to Lucy Gubbin and Brigit Viney, whose comments on different drafts of this book were invaluable, and to Sarah Almy at Cambridge University Press for her guidance and support. Thanks also to Mary Spratt and Steven Miller at Cambridge ESOL, who provided useful suggestions on early drafts of this book and helped me develop as an item writer for the TKT: KAL. Finally, thank you to Gavin Jones, whose patience, encouragement and support were essential when writing this book.
David Albery

The authors and publishers acknowledge the following sources of copyright material and are grateful for the permissions granted. While every effort has been made, it has not always been possible to identify the sources of all the material used, or to trace all copyright holders. If any omissions are brought to our notice, we will be happy to include the appropriate acknowledgements on reprinting.

Phonemic Chart on p. 30 from *Sound Foundations* by Adrian Underhill, copyright © Adrian Underhill 1994, reproduced by permission of Macmillan Education; Sample Sheet on p. 114 reproduced with permission from Cambridge ESOL.

The publisher has used its best endeavours to ensure that the URLs for external websites referred to in this book are correct and active at the time of going to press. However, the publisher has no responsibility for the websites and can make no guarantee that a site will remain live or that the content is or will remain appropriate.

Introduction

■ What is the Teaching Knowledge Test: Knowledge About Language (the TKT: KAL)?

The *Teaching Knowledge Test: Knowledge About Language* (the TKT: KAL) is a specialist module of the *Teaching Knowledge Test* (the TKT) developed by Cambridge ESOL. The TKT: KAL is for new or experienced teachers of English working with young and adult learners in primary and secondary schools and colleges.

The TKT: KAL tests candidates' knowledge of the systems of the English language needed by teachers for planning and teaching their lessons. TKT: KAL does NOT test candidates' English language proficiency, their knowledge of teaching methodology or their practical teaching skills.

The TKT: KAL consists of one module. There are 80 objective questions in the test. The task types are: matching, multiple choice and finding the odd one out.

The test is divided into four parts, each part testing candidates' knowledge of one of the systems of English (lexis, phonology, grammar and discourse) as well as their awareness of the linguistic problems faced by students when learning English, such as problems with forming different grammatical structures, or pronouncing different sounds.

The TKT: KAL has no entry requirements such as previous teaching experience or teaching qualifications. Candidates are recommended to have *at least* an upper intermediate level of English (e.g. Level B2 of the Council of Europe's Common European Framework of Reference for Languages (CEFR) or IELTS band 5.5). They are expected to be familiar with key English language concepts and language terms included in the *TKT Glossary*. (This includes terms for the TKT: KAL.) The *TKT Glossary* is available on the Cambridge ESOL website at:
http://www.cambridgeesol.org/exams/teaching-awards/tkt.html

■ What is *The TKT Course KAL Module*?

The TKT Course KAL Module is a course to prepare candidates to take the TKT: KAL. It has three main aims:

1 to introduce readers to the concepts and terms related to English that are important for teachers and for the TKT: KAL test
2 to provide practice with TKT: KAL sample tasks and a test paper
3 to provide materials and activities that give teachers opportunities to develop professionally by extending their knowledge about English.

■ Who is *The TKT Course KAL Module* written for?

The TKT Course KAL Module is written for the following readers:

- candidates preparing for the TKT: KAL
- teacher trainers preparing candidates for the TKT: KAL
- pre-service or in-service teachers of ESOL revising or extending their knowledge of English
- teacher trainers developing trainees' knowledge of English
- both non-native and native speakers of English.

As the TKT (including the KAL module) is described by Cambridge ESOL as catering for a range of candidates extending from those who are in pre-service training to experienced teachers, readers from the following backgrounds may also benefit from using this course:

- teachers preparing for other teaching awards (CELTA, Delta, etc.)
- teachers who have completed an initial teaching award and now want to find out more about English.

■ What are the contents of *The TKT Course KAL Module*?

The TKT Course KAL Module mostly follows the content and order of the TKT: KAL syllabus. The order of items in the syllabus has been changed at times to allow the reader to process information more easily.

The book consists of four parts: Lexis; Phonology; Grammar; Discourse. These mirror the four parts of the TKT: KAL test and are in the same order as the test. Each part is divided into units which cover the TKT: KAL syllabus for that part.

The book also contains:

- many ELT and KAL terms from the *TKT Glossary*. These are highlighted in bold the first time they occur in a unit. Most are defined in the book and all are defined in the *TKT Glossary*.
- terms that readers will also find useful when revising and extending their knowledge about language but which are not in the *TKT Glossary*. All are defined in the book.
- a TKT: KAL practice test
- exam tips for taking the TKT: KAL
- answer keys for the Exercises and the Follow-up activities. These also include further notes on the topic of the unit.
- answer keys for the TKT: KAL practice tasks and practice test
- an alphabetical list of terms from the *TKT Glossary*
- a unit-by-unit list of terms from the *TKT Glossary*.

How is each part organised and how can it be used?

This book can be used by self-access learners or by learners on a taught course. It can easily be adapted for use by teacher trainers.

Each of the four parts of the book begins with a starter question, such as 'What is lexis?', and an answer. The answer provides a definition of the title of each part. The parts are then divided into units.

The table below summarises how each unit is organised.

Section	Purposes	Suggestions for use
Learning outcome	To inform readers of the knowledge they should have after completing the unit.	Read this before you start the unit and again when you have finished. Have you achieved the outcome? What do you need to look at again?
Input section (the main part of the unit that contains information)	To introduce the main ideas of the unit and key terms.	The input section includes a number of exercises (see below). Make sure you do them as you read. They will help you understand the information in the unit more fully.
Exercises (these appear in the input section)	To guide readers through the input section. To encourage readers to work out the main ideas themselves and so aid understanding. To reinforce what readers already know and to highlight what they do not yet know. To allow readers to reflect on what they have just learnt. To provide examples of the main areas covered. To provide additional practice of areas covered in the TKT: KAL syllabus.	Try to complete each exercise before referring to the Answer key (see pages 116–32). Make sure you read any additional notes in the Answer key. If you are on a course or working with a group of teachers, you could do these exercises with others, helping one another to learn more about the area of language.
Follow-up activities	To provide practice of some areas covered in the input section and to highlight what has been learnt and what may need more attention.	It is important to do these so that you have a better awareness of what areas you need to revise and which you are familiar with. The Answer key to these activities is also on pages 116–32.

Section	Purposes	Suggestions for use
Discovery activities	To encourage readers to find out more about the areas covered in the input section and to relate these areas to their own development and to teaching.	The extra research involved in these activities will help you develop your knowledge about language further.
TKT: KAL practice task	To review some of the unit's content and to help readers become more familiar with task formats used in the test.	Do the whole task before checking your answers in the Answer key on page 133. This will give you a good idea of which areas you need to look at again.

We recommend readers refer to the *TKT Glossary* as they read the book, and familiarise themselves with the definitions for terms introduced in each unit. Readers will also find it useful to have access to a good grammar reference while using the book, and a good dictionary such as the *Cambridge Advanced Learner's Dictionary (Third Edition)*.

For more information about the TKT: KAL go to:
http://www.cambridgeesol.org/exams/tkt/index.html#tktkl

Part 1 | Lexis

What is lexis?

Lexis (or **vocabulary**) refers to single words, or sets of words, that have a specific meaning, for example: *car, pick up, in the end*.

Unit 1   Types of meaning

> **LEARNING OUTCOME**
>
> KNOWLEDGE: the different types of meaning that items of lexis can have and the terms used to describe these

■ What affects the meaning of items of lexis?

Items of **lexis** have different types of meaning depending on the situation or **context** they are used in, what **function** (purpose for communication, e.g. giving advice) they perform and who is using them.

■ Denotation and connotation

> **Exercise 1**
>
> What is the meaning of the underlined words in the sentences below? When you have thought about the meaning, read the next section.
>
> 1 Shall we sit at the table?
> 2 I'm trying to give up chocolate.
> 3 I'm going to take my books to school.
> 4 He's really skinny. I think he may be ill.
> 5 This film is so boring!

The meaning of *table* in number 1 above is 'a flat surface, usually supported by four legs, used for putting things on' (from the *Cambridge Advanced Learner's Dictionary (Third Edition)*). The meaning given in a dictionary is called the **denotation** (or sometimes the **literal meaning**). Literal meaning also refers to the original or basic meaning of a word or group of words (see also the section on figurative meaning on pages 6–7). Sometimes the denotation of individual words is obvious as in *table* in number 1 above, or *take* in number 3. At other times the denotation of a combination of words may be more difficult to understand as in *give up* in number 2 above. In this example of a **multiword verb** (a verb plus an **adverb/preposition particle**), the separate denotations of *give* and *up* do not give the meaning of *give up*. It is sometimes important to look at words in combination when understanding their meaning.

Look again at number 4 in Exercise 1. The denotation of the word *skinny* is 'very thin' but it has an additional negative meaning: an idea that is suggested by the word. This is called the **connotation**. So, the full meaning of *skinny* is 'very thin (denotation) in a bad way (connotation)'. Words or sets of words can have a negative, a positive or a neutral connotation. Some dictionaries provide information about connotations. For example, the *Cambridge Advanced Learner's Dictionary (Third Edition)* says that *skinny* is 'MAINLY DISAPPROVING'. Sometimes, it is the denotation itself that has a negative meaning, for example *boring* in number 5 in Exercise 1.

Because some words have negative connotations or denotations, people often avoid them by using other words or phrases. For example, they might use *very slim* because it is more positive than *skinny*. Sometimes people 'soften' words by adding others. For example, *It was a bit boring* is more positive than *It was boring*.

Exercise 2

Is the denotation or connotation of the underlined words below different from their denotation or connotation in Exercise 1?

1   In business reports, it's common to use <u>tables</u> and graphs.
2   I <u>gave up</u> ice-cream last year and feel so much healthier.
3   I usually <u>take</u> the bus to work.
4   He's as <u>skinny</u> as he was when he was 16. He looks great!

Check your answers on page 116.

In English, many words can be used with different meanings. Some words (e.g. *table*) can change their meaning because they are used for different things. Some can 'lose' their meaning. For example, *take* has a denotation of 'move from one place to another' but in number 3 in Exercise 2, it has 'lost' this meaning without gaining another. This is because it is part of the **collocation** *take a bus*, i.e. the words *take* and *bus* regularly go together and the meaning of *take* cannot be separated from *bus*. Verbs that 'lose' their meaning in this way are called **delexicalised** verbs. Another example is *have* in *I have a shower every morning* (which does not mean 'possess or own a shower'). (For more information on collocations, see pages 20–1, Unit 4.)

The connotation of a word can also change according to the situation or the context it is used in or the person using it. For example, in number 4 above, although *skinny* often has a negative connotation, the speaker is using it in a positive way. When using lexis it is important to make sure you understand the denotation, the generally accepted connotation and also the specific connotation in the context in which it is being used.

■ Figurative meaning

The term **figurative** is used to describe words or sets of words whose meaning is non-literal and imaginative. For example: *I could eat a horse* means 'I'm extremely hungry', *they received a flood of letters* means 'they received a lot of letters all at once' and *he can swim like a fish* means 'he can swim very well'. In order to find the meaning of a figurative phrase in a dictionary, decide which word is key and look for this in the dictionary. For example, *eat* is key in the first example above.

Exercise 3

Look at the underlined words in the sentences below and complete the table. The first one has been done for you.

Why do the speakers here use this kind of figurative language?

Words / Sets of words	Literal meaning	Figurative meaning
1 I ate so much I thought I was going to <u>burst</u>.	Explode like a balloon.	I felt extremely full.
2 She has <u>the voice of an angel</u>.		
3 He has such <u>a sunny smile</u>.		
4 We were <u>baking</u>. The weather was so hot.		

Check your answers on page 116.

In number 1 you can guess the figurative meaning of *burst* here by relating the denotation to the context. For example, *burst* means 'explode because something is very full, like a balloon'. Here it is describing the feeling of being about to explode because you have eaten a lot.

Some figurative phrases are called **idioms**. (For more information on idioms, see page 21, Unit 4.)

■ Register

Exercise 4

Look at the dictionary entry below for the word *drill*.

drill /drɪl/   *noun* [C]

1 a tool or machine which makes holes

(*Cambridge Advanced Learner's Dictionary (Third Edition)*, Cambridge University Press 2008)

Now look at *drill* in the sentence below. Is the meaning the same as above?

When I teach I like to drill my students by getting them to repeat words two or three times, so they can practise and remember the pronunciation.

The word *drill* has changed its meaning in the sentence because it is being used by a particular person (a teacher) to mean 'ordered and controlled repetition of language'. The set of words used by particular groups of people (e.g. people who have the same jobs, are of the same age, belong to the same social group) is called **register**. As with *drill*, this can mean that a word can change its meaning, or that a different word is used instead of a more common one. For example, *leave* means the same as *depart* but *depart* is perhaps more commonly used in the register of public transport services.

Register and **style** (a typical way of conveying information, e.g. business-like or casual) also refer to the kind of words used in a particular kind of text, for example a letter of complaint or a relaxed chat at a party. This may involve using **formal** or **informal** (also called **colloquial**) words. For example, we expect a formal speech to begin with *Good morning/evening/afternoon* rather than *Hi*. The function (i.e. greeting) remains the same but because *Hi* is not the right register for a formal speech, it is used wrongly in this context.

You can often find out what register a word or set of words is by looking in a good English dictionary, such as the *Cambridge Advanced Learner's Dictionary (Third Edition)*. Entries in this dictionary will tell you if a word is formal or informal. For example: 'hi *exclamation INFORMAL*'. The definitions given in a dictionary will often tell you if a word is used by a particular group of people. For example, *drill* is associated with the military, which leads to the meaning teachers give it.

FOLLOW-UP ACTIVITIES *(See page 116 for answers)*

1 Look at the underlined items of lexis in the table below and make notes about the meaning and register of each one.

Item of lexis	Figurative? Meaning?	Register
1 Last Sunday was <u>boiling</u> hot!		
2 <u>I would appreciate it if</u> you could …		
3 Overwork can lead to serious <u>fatigue</u>.		
4 So, <u>how's it going</u>?		
5 See you soon. <u>Tons of love</u>, Anne		

2 Look at the underlined items of lexis in the sentences below. How does their meaning change from sentence a) to sentence b)?
   1 a) Could you <u>pick up</u> that pen for me?
     b) If you've got the car, could you <u>pick</u> me <u>up</u>?
   2 a) I had <u>chips</u> for my dinner.
     b) How many <u>chips</u> are in a computer?
   3 a) I <u>went</u> to the cinema last Saturday.
     b) I nearly <u>went</u> mad trying to do my homework.

DISCOVERY ACTIVITIES

1 Find a text (e.g. a newspaper article, a reading text from a student's English coursebook). Underline any words and phrases which have a figurative meaning. Use a dictionary if necessary.
2 Choose five words you taught your students recently. Use a dictionary to find out if they have other meanings, what their register is, whether they can be used figuratively and if they have any particular connotations.

....

TKT: KAL practice task 1 *(See page 133 for answers)*

A teacher is writing comments about her students' use of lexis.

For questions **1-6**, match the students' sentences with the teacher's comments listed **A-G**.

There is one extra option you do not need to use.

Teacher's comments

> **A** You've got the right idea but the wrong register. We use *departure gate* in this context.
>
> **B** This phrase is too formal for this situation. You need a more informal phrase.
>
> **C** Good. You chose the right verb–noun collocation. Notice how the verb changes its meaning.
>
> **D** This word is too informal in this context. Do you know a more formal equivalent?
>
> **E** This word is very strange in this sentence. Is it a spelling mistake?
>
> **F** Good to see you using figurative language but in English this doesn't collocate.
>
> **G** This word generally has a negative connotation. Find one with a positive connotation.

Students' sentences

1 How do you do, Katy? Happy anniversary! Give me a kiss!
2 I usually take a break at about 11 o'clock.
3 Where's the door for getting to the plane?
4 You're looking burnt from the sun! You look wonderful!
5 I am writing to complain about the behaviour of some kids at my local school.
6 That's really kind of you. Thanks a thousand.

....

Unit 2   Sense relations

LEARNING OUTCOME

KNOWLEDGE: how words relate to one another in meaning and the terms used to describe these different kinds of relationship

■ What are sense relations?

Sense relations are the relationships between words based on the words' meanings, for example the relationship between *flower* and *rose,* or between *hot* and *cold*.

■ Lexical sets, hyponyms and superordinates

Exercise 1

Look at the lists below. What is the relationship between the words and phrases in each list?

1   book, pen, teacher, whiteboard, student, desk, do your homework
2   menu, waiter, book a table, main course, tip

Now read the next section.

A group of words or phrases that is linked by a common **topic** or situation is called a **lexical set**. In Exercise 1, the words and phrases in number 1 are linked by the topic of *school* and in number 2 they are linked by *restaurant*.

Exercise 2

Look at the lists below. What is the relationship between the underlined word in each list and the other words in that list?

1   <u>furniture</u>, table, chair, sofa, bed
2   potato, carrot, <u>vegetable</u>, cabbage, bean

Check your answers on page 116.

The words which are underlined are called **superordinates** and the words which are not underlined are called **hyponyms**. For example, *chair* is a hyponym of *furniture* and *vegetable* is the superordinate of *potato, carrot, cabbage* and *bean*. Hyponyms can become superordinates and vice versa depending on the groups they are listed in. For example, *table* can be the superordinate of *desk* and *breakfast counter* while *vegetable* could be a hyponym of *food*.

Hyponyms and superordinates are often used when writing or speaking in order not to repeat the same word, for example: *All there was to eat were apples, bananas and oranges; it was lucky I liked fruit.* Here the superordinate has been used to replace the hyponyms. They can also be used to give a text 'lexical cohesion', i.e. to connect parts of the text lexically. (For information on lexical cohesion, see page 90, Unit 16.)

Dictionary definitions often make use of hyponyms, superordinates and the relationship between them.

Exercise 3

Look at the definitions below (which are based on those in the *Cambridge Advanced Learner's Dictionary (Third Edition)*). Underline the superordinates and circle the hyponyms in each.

1   A horse is a large animal with four legs which people ride on.
2   Clothes are things such as dresses and trousers that you wear to cover your body.
3   A car is a road vehicle with an engine, four wheels and seats.
4   A container is an object such as a box or a bottle which can be used for holding something.

Check your answers on page 117.

■ ## Homonyms, homophones and homographs

Exercise 4

Look at the pairs of words below. What is similar about the words in each pair? What is different about them?

1   flat (apartment), flat (smooth)
2   sea, see
3   close (verb), close (adjective)

Check your answers on page 117.

The words in each pair above are similar in some ways – they have the same spelling and/or pronunciation – but they have different meanings. **Homonyms** are words which have the same spelling and pronunciation but different meanings (number 1). **Homophones** are words which have the same pronunciation but different meanings and spellings (number 2). Homographs are words that have the same spelling but a different pronunciation and meaning (number 3).

■ ## False friends

Sometimes an English word has the same, or similar, spelling and/or sound as a word in another language but it has a different meaning. This can be a problem for learners because they may misunderstand the English word. For example, in English a *library* is somewhere you can borrow (not buy) a book but in Spanish a *libreria* is somewhere you can buy (not borrow) a book (a *bookshop* in English). We call both the English and Spanish words **false friends** or false cognates.

Sometimes an English word has the same, or similar, spelling and/or sound as a word in another language *and* it has the same meaning. (The two words often come from the same word in a different language.) These words are called cognates and are, in a way, the opposite of false friends. Examples of cognates in some languages are *hospital*, *television* and *police*. Can you think of any false friends and cognates that occur between English and other languages?

■ Synonyms and antonyms

Exercise 5

Look at the sets of words below. Decide what the relationship is between the words in each set.

1 good, nice, satisfactory, enjoyable, pleasant   4 hot, freezing
2 borrow, lend   5 good, bad
3 chat, talk, discuss

Check your answers on page 117.

Synonyms are words that have the same or similar meaning, for example: *begin, start* and *commence* or *below* and *under*. Dictionaries often make use of synonyms in their definitions. Many synonyms do not have exactly the same meaning. For example, in number 3 above, *chat* is not exactly the same as *talk* or *discuss* because it is **informal** and means 'to talk in a friendly way'. You *chat* with a friend but *talk* to the police and you *discuss* something serious but *chat* about something that is not so serious.

Synonyms may differ in **connotation**, **register** and the range of **contexts** in which they are used. For example, *chair* and *seat* can be synonyms: *Is that chair/seat comfortable?* However, *seat* can be used in a wide range of contexts (a seat in class, in the theatre, on a train, in the kitchen) whereas *chair* is not normally used in the theatre or on a train. *Thin* and *skinny* are synonyms, as we saw in Unit 1, but *skinny* often has a negative connotation while *thin* is neutral.

Different words with the same meaning are used in different **varieties of English**, for example: *biscuit* (UK) and *cookie* (US); *illness* (general use) and *condition* (medical); *Awesome!* and *Lovely!* (different ages and social groups will prefer to use one or the other). Some words are more **formal** or informal than their synonyms, for example: *I do hope we meet again soon* (formal situations) and *See you later* (informal situations).

Words that have opposite meanings are called **antonyms**. In Exercise 5, number 5, *good* and *bad* are true opposites and one excludes the other. If something is *good* it cannot be *bad*; *good* can replace *bad* with an opposite meaning. However, antonyms are not always truly opposite. For example, in number 2, *borrow* cannot replace *lend* with an opposite meaning. That is, *borrow* does not mean *not lend* in the way that *good* means *not bad*. The 'opposite' of *I borrowed the book* is *I didn't borrow the book* not *I lent the book*. In number 4, *hot* and *freezing* are near opposites and are on a scale of *heat*, with *boiling* at the opposite end of the scale from *freezing*.

As we saw in Unit 1, some words have more than one meaning, which means that they have more than one antonym. For example, in *This bag is so light and easy to carry*, the opposite of *light* is *heavy*. However, in *My bedroom is very light in the mornings*, the opposite of *light* is *dark*.

FOLLOW-UP ACTIVITIES *(See page 117 for answers)*

1 What is the sense relation of each of the sets of words below?
   1 car, lorry, train, bus   4 their, they're, there
   2 apple, orange, fruit, strawberry   5 same, different; big, small; give, take
   3 like, be keen on, love, adore   6 bright, cloudy, stupid, dark

2 Choose words or phrases from the box for 1–6.

> watch TV   little   record (verb)   eye   see a film   vegetable   sport
> house   go out for dinner   end

   1 a synonym of *finish*   4 a hyponym of *building*
   2 three phrases that make a lexical set   5 a homophone of *I*
   3 a superordinate of *football, tennis* and *baseball*   6 an antonym of *big*

DISCOVERY ACTIVITIES

1 Find a text (e.g. a newspaper article). Find examples of synonyms, antonyms, homonyms, superordinates, hyponyms and lexical sets.
2 Look at Chapter 1 of *How to Teach Vocabulary* by Scott Thornbury, Pearson Education Ltd 2002. What else can you learn about synonyms, antonyms, homonyms, superordinates, hyponyms and lexical sets from this chapter?

TKT: KAL practice task 2 *(See page 133 for answers)*

A teacher is researching ways of describing sets of words and phrases.

For questions **1-7**, match the sets of words with the lexical terms that best describe them listed **A-D**.

You need to use some options more than once.

Lexical terms

A homophones
B synonyms
C a lexical set
D antonyms

Sets of words and phrases
1 dislike, love; leave, arrive
2 beach, sun, sand, sea
3 through, threw; no, know
4 pen, computer, desk, phone
5 so, therefore; speak, talk
6 their, they're; new, knew
7 football, baseball, swimming

Unit 3   Word formation

LEARNING OUTCOME

KNOWLEDGE: how some words can be formed from others and how a word's form affects its meaning and shows its part of speech, and key terms used to describe these topics

■ Morphemes and affixation

A **morpheme** is the smallest unit that has meaning in a language. For example, the word *cat* has one morpheme but the word *cats* has two: *cat* and *s*. Both *cat* and *s* have meaning (*cat* means 'a small furry animal with four legs and a tail', and *s* means 'more than one') but you cannot divide *cat* and keep any meaning.

Some morphemes can exist as words on their own (e.g. *cat*) but others cannot (e.g. *s*). Morphemes that can exist alone and still have meaning are called free morphemes, while those that cannot are called bound morphemes.

Exercise 1

How many morphemes are there in the words below? Which are free? Which are bound?

1 unattractive
2 midday
3 movement
4 teachers

Check your answers on page 117.

A morpheme is often added to the beginning or end of a word to form a word that has a different meaning or is a different part of speech from the original.

Exercise 2

How do the morphemes in Exercise 1 change the words *attract*, *day*, *move* and *teach*? For example, *un* changes the meaning of *attractive* to the opposite of *attractive*.

Check your answers on page 117.

Morphemes that are added at the beginning of words are called **prefixes** and those at the end are called **suffixes**. They are both types of **affixes** and the process of adding affixes is **affixation**. Prefixes normally change the meaning of a word (e.g. <u>un</u>*happy*) while suffixes normally change the **part of speech** of a word (e.g. when *er* is added to *teach* the **verb** changes to a **noun**).

Exercise 3

Complete the table below by adding words to the columns. In the fourth column, add a negative prefix to the adjective(s) from the third column. Sometimes there is no word you can add to a space.

Verb	Noun	Adjective	Negative prefix + adjective
employ			
		possible	impossible
depend			
	economy		
record			

Check your answers by reading Tables 1 and 2 and the table on page 117.

Table 1 below shows common suffixes and the parts of speech they often make. Table 2 on page 16 shows common prefixes and their most common meanings.

Table 1 Suffixes

Suffixes – nouns	Examples	Suffixes – adjectives	Examples
-al	arrival	-able	recordable
-ant, -ent	assistant, student	-atic	systematic
-dom	boredom, freedom	-ed	employed
-ee	employee	-ent	dependent
-ence	dependence	-ful	helpful
-er, -or	teacher, instructor	-ic(al)	economic(al)
-hood	childhood	-ish	brownish
-ity	possibility	-ive	productive
-ment	employment	-less	careless
-ness	happiness	-ous	famous
-tion	production	-y	windy
Suffixes – verbs	**Examples**	**Suffixes – adverbs**	**Examples**
-ate	originate	-ly	quickly
-ise	economise	-wards	afterwards

Knowledge of how suffixes form words can help us identify parts of speech. For example, when we see an *-ate* ending, we know the word is likely to be a verb. (For examples of how suffixes can affect words in other ways, see page 25, Unit 5.)

Table 2 Prefixes

Prefixes	Meanings	Examples
anti-	opposed to, against	anti-social
dis-	the opposite of	disagree, dishonest, distrust
extra-	outside, in addition to	extraordinary
il-, im-, in-	not	illegal, impossible, inexperienced
inter-	between, among	international
mid-	in the middle of	midday, midnight, mid-December
mis-	wrong, wrongly, bad, badly	misspelling, misspell, misbehaviour, misbehave
non-	not	non-stop, non-recordable
over-	too much	overeat, overweight
pre-	before	pre-heat, pre-arrange
re-	again	remake, rewrite, reunite
un-	not, lacking, the opposite of	undress, unlucky, unrecorded
under-	not enough	underachieve, underweight

However, sometimes a word looks as if it has a prefix when in fact it does not. For example, *record* or *resign* do not have the meaning of 'again'. The verb *record* does not mean 'cord again'; there is no verb *cord* in English.

■ Spelling rules

> ### Exercise 4
> Look at the words below. How has the spelling changed from the base word in brackets, and why?
>
> 1 (happy) happiness
> 2 (advise) advisable
> 3 (complete) completely
>
> Check your answers and read the notes on page 118.

When adding prefixes and suffixes, there are a number of spelling rules that need to be followed (see Table 3 below for a selection). However, there are often exceptions to these rules and a number of irregular **forms**.

Table 3 Spelling rules for affixes

Spelling rule	Examples
When prefixes are added, letters are not normally added or taken away.	(sure) unsure, (necessary) unnecessary
When the first letter of a word is *l*, *p* or *r*, the negative prefix is often *il-*, *im-* and *ir-*.	(legal) illegal, (possible) impossible, (responsible) irresponsible
The final consonant of a word is often doubled when a suffix beginning with a vowel is added.	(fit) fitting, (drop) dropped
When a suffix beginning with a vowel is added to a word ending in *e*, the *e* is normally dropped.	(invite) invitation, (fame) famous

Spelling rule	Examples
When a suffix beginning with a consonant is added to a word ending in *e*, the *e* is not normally dropped.	(wide) widely, (blame) blameless
When a suffix is added to a word ending in a consonant plus *y*, the *y* normally changes to *i*.	(empty) emptiness, (easy) easily

(based on *Cambridge Grammar of English* by Ronald Carter and Michael McCarthy, Cambridge University Press 2006)

■ Word families

Look again at the table you completed in Exercise 3. These lists of words are called **word families**. They are the parts of speech formed from a single **root word** or **base word**. For example, *employment* (noun), *employed* (**adjective**) and *employable* (adjective) are all part of the word family formed from the root word *employ*.

Exercise 5

Write word families for the words below. Use a dictionary if necessary.

1 believe   2 create

Check your answers on page 118.

■ Compounds

Exercise 6

Look at 1–4 in the table below. How many words are in each?

	Number of words
1 ice cream	
2 nice-looking	
3 dry clean	
4 homework	

Check your answers and read the notes on page 118.

New words can be formed by combining two or more words, for example *ice cream*. Both *ice* and *cream* have their own meaning but a new word with a new meaning is created by combining them. We call this a **compound**.

Compound pattern	Examples
noun + noun	ice cream, homework
noun + adjective	homesick, oven ready
verb + **particle**	wake up, find out
adjective + verb	wet shave, dry clean

Compound pattern	Examples
adjective/**adverb** + **past/present participle**	good-tempered, nice-looking, well-spoken, hard-working
preposition + preposition	into, onto, upon

Compounds can be different parts of speech. For example, *ice cream* is a noun, *homesick* is an adjective and *into* is a compound preposition.

■ Types of abbreviations and acronyms

Exercise 7

What is the full form of the words below?

1 wasn't   2 DVD   3 advert   4 RAM

Check your answers and read the notes on page 118.

The types of **abbreviations** (short forms of words) in the boxes above are common in English and are used in both speaking and writing. *Wasn't* is a **contraction**, i.e. a shorter form of two words which have been joined together, with an **apostrophe** replacing any letters that have been missed out. Contractions are perhaps more common in speaking and are associated with an informal **register**. Some abbreviations (e.g. *DVD* and *RAM*) are used so commonly that they have replaced the full form and many people do not know what the full form is. Some are used more in certain varieties of English. For example, *advert* is perhaps more common in British than American English. Abbreviations such as *RAM*, which are made from the first letters of the full term but are pronounced as single words, are called **acronyms**. Acronyms are commonly used for governmental and (semi-)political organisations (e.g. *UNESCO*). Abbreviations such as *DVD*, in which the letters are pronounced separately, are called **initialisms**. A good dictionary will normally list abbreviations as items on their own rather than, or as well as, under their full form.

FOLLOW-UP ACTIVITIES *(See page 118 for answers)*

1 Identify the affixes in the following words.
   1 interdependent   2 underachiever   3 unproductive   4 disagreement

2 Look at the words in the box and find an example of the words described in 1–4. You do not need to use all the words in the box.

socialise	get up	interpersonal	swimmer	overheat	cooker	car park

   1 an adjective with a prefix and a suffix
   2 a word with a suffix which means 'person who'
   3 a compound noun
   4 a word with a verb suffix

DISCOVERY ACTIVITIES

1 Find a text (e.g. a newspaper article). Find examples of words with affixes. Then use a dictionary to find out if other affixes can be used with these words.

2 Look at the section 'Word structure and word formation' in *Cambridge Grammar of English* by Ronald Carter and Michael McCarthy, Cambridge University Press 2006. What more can you find out about word formation?

TKT: KAL practice task 3 *(See page 133 for answers)*

A teacher is commenting on her students' written and spoken sentences.

For questions **1-6**, match the students' sentences with the comments listed **A-G**.

There is one extra option which you do not need to use.

Teacher's comments

A You've used the wrong prefix in this adjective.
B You could use an abbreviation here instead of this word.
C You don't need to drop the *e* before a suffix beginning with a consonant.
D You need to add a suffix here to make the correct noun.
E You could use a contraction here because it's informal.
F You probably shouldn't use a contraction in this formal situation.
G You need to double the consonant before this suffix.

Sentences

1 I'm living at 22 Brent Street.
2 That's really unprobable.
3 Dear Mr Smith, I'm writing to apply for the …
4 I want to be a computer programme when I leave school.
5 I will not be there on Saturday. Sorry, Jane.
6 What's all the noise, kids? Why so much excitment?

Unit 4   Lexical units

LEARNING OUTCOME

KNOWLEDGE: how words combine with other words in different ways (e.g. with one other word or with more than one to make a complete phrase), and key terms associated with this area

■ What are lexical units?

Words can combine with other words. For example, in Unit 3 we saw that words can combine to make compounds. Combinations of words are sometimes called lexical units.

■ Collocations

Exercise 1
Look at the table below and decide which adjectives can be used with which nouns. (Some adjectives can combine with more than one noun.)

Adjective	Noun
heavy	wind
strong	sunshine
light	snow

Check your answers on page 118.

A pair or group of words that regularly appear together is called a **collocation**. For example, *heavy snow* and *strong wind* are collocations while *heavy wind* is not. The fact that these words appear together so regularly cannot simply be chance and so we say that the words **collocate** with each other.

Words which combine with each other but not with very many other words are called strong collocators and form strong collocations. For example, the **adverb** *strongly* collocates with *recommend, advise* and *agree* but with few other **verbs**, so *strongly recommend/advise/agree* are strong collocations. Those that combine with a large number of other words are weak collocators and form weak collocations. Generally, the more common a word is, the weaker the collocations it forms.

Register can affect collocation. For example, in the register of the police you would probably find that *examine evidence* is a strong collocation, while in a more general use you would probably find *look at/think about information/evidence* is more common.

Exercise 2

Look at the table below and decide which verbs collocate with which nouns. What meaning does the verb have in each collocation?

Verb	Noun
go	a pill
	home
catch	mad
take	a bus
	a ball

Check your answers on page 118.

Words can change their meaning depending on the collocation. For example, in *go home* the verb means 'travel' but in *go mad* it means 'become'. The best way to decide the meaning of common verbs such as *go, catch* and *take* is to look at the **context** they are used in (the situation or the words before and after a particular word). A good dictionary will list the collocations of common words.

■ Idioms

Idioms are phrases which use fixed words in a fixed order and in which the meaning of the individual words does not give you the meaning of the phrase; the meaning is **figurative** or **idiomatic**. For example, *I need to pick your brains* means 'I need to ask you for information about something you know about'.

You can often guess the meaning of an idiom from the context it is used in. If you use a dictionary, you should decide which word in the phrase is key. For example, *pick* and *brain* are key in the idiom above. However, it can be hard to identify which words are key in an idiom and some dictionaries use references to all key words. Idioms are normally clearly identified in dictionaries, for example '[IDIOM]'.

Exercise 3

Read the passage below and underline the idioms. What does each idiom mean?

> I was in the supermarket the other day when this man caught my eye. He came over and asked me to give him a hand carrying his bags to the car. Well, we were just leaving when a shop assistant asked to look in the bags. Full of stolen food! I couldn't believe my eyes! And he nearly died when I told him I'm a police officer and arrested him. I hope he's learnt his lesson … but I don't suppose he has.

Which parts of the idioms above can change? For example, can the verbs or the pronouns change?

Check your answers and read the notes on page 119.

Idioms are not used frequently. They are almost always used in an **informal** register.

■ Formulaic phrases

We saw in the previous section that the word order of idioms does not normally change but that some parts such as the **pronouns** and **tenses** can change. These are called semi-fixed phrases because some parts change depending on the context they are used in. In a fixed phrase, on the other hand, none of the parts ever changes. For example, *How do you do?* and *That's that!* are fixed phrases. There are a large number of fixed and semi-fixed phrases in English and many of them have a **literal** rather than a figurative meaning. Fixed and semi-fixed phrases are sometimes called formulaic phrases because they follow set patterns of form. Formulaic phrases and collocations are also sometimes called **chunks**.

Exercise 4

Which of the underlined formulaic phrases below are fixed and which are semi-fixed?

1 See you soon!
2 You can't be serious!
3 To whom it may concern.
4 Would you like some fish and chips?
5 That's not the best way of doing it, if you ask me.
6 You'd better leave before you miss your train.

Check your answers on page 119.

Many formulaic phrases have a social function (something which creates or manages relationships) or are used in **discourse** (spoken or written language in longer texts). For example, *Have a nice day* (a fixed phrase) is used as a friendly ending to a conversation and *if you ask me* (a fixed phrase) is used to show that what you have said or are going to say is your opinion.

As with idioms, it is usually better to look at the meaning of the whole formulaic phrase rather than break it into smaller pieces. Many formulaic phrases will be listed in a good dictionary and you need to decide which is the key word and then look for this in the dictionary. For example, *How do you do?* is listed in the *Cambridge Advanced Learner's Dictionary (Third Edition)* under the key word *how*.

FOLLOW-UP ACTIVITIES *(See page 119 for answers)*

1 Match the verbs and nouns below to form common collocations.

Verb	Noun
1 have	a mistake
2 make	a headache
3 do	a train
4 catch	exercise

2 Are the statements below about idioms true or false?
  1 Idioms have a literal meaning.
  2 All idioms are fixed phrases.
  3 Idioms are used very frequently in English.
  4 Idioms are often used in informal situations.
  5 The word order in an idiom is normally fixed.

DISCOVERY ACTIVITIES

1 Look at two or three coursebooks and find out if they teach vocabulary in formulaic phrases. Which formulaic phrases do/could they teach for speaking and for writing?

2 Make a list of words you have taught your learners recently. Think of common collocations, using as many of these words as possible. To find more collocations, you could look in a collocations dictionary such as the *Oxford Collocations Dictionary for Students of English* by C. McIntosh, B. Francis and R. Poole, Oxford University Press 2009.

TKT: KAL practice task 4 *(See page 133 for answers)*

A teacher is doing some research on words that are often found together.

For questions **1-6**, answer the questions about the text by choosing the correct option **A**, **B** or **C**.

Text

Hi Janey	line 1
Been here just over a week and there's been nothing but heavy rain	line 2
so far. On the second day I caught a cold but kept working and now	line 3
feel utterly exhausted. The trouble is, all the kids depend on me so I	line 4
have to keep going. The school keeps asking me to stay another	line 5
week. They must be joking! So, hopefully I'll be back on Saturday.	line 6
Lots of love	line 7
David	line 8

Questions

1 Which line contains a verb + noun collocation?
   A line 2   **B** line 3   **C** line 4
2 Which line contains a semi-fixed phrase?
   A line 2   **B** line 5   **C** line 6
3 Which line contains a verb + preposition collocation?
   A line 3   **B** line 4   **C** line 7
4 Which line contains an adjective + noun collocation?
   A line 2   **B** line 4   **C** line 5
5 Which line contains a fixed phrase?
   A line 1   **B** line 3   **C** line 7
6 Which line contains an adverb + adjective collocation?
   A line 3   **B** line 4   **C** line 6

Unit 5   Lexico-grammatical features

LEARNING OUTCOME

KNOWLEDGE: how morphemes function in words, how words function in a sentence and combine with other words grammatically, and key terms associated with this area

■ What are lexico-grammatical features?

'Lexico-grammatical' is a term often used to refer to grammatical **features** of **lexis**. For example, the **morpheme** *s* in the lexical item *tables* is a feature that can be described grammatically, i.e. it is a plural *s* morpheme.

Other lexico-grammatical features include the grammatical function of words and their position in a sentence (e.g. **adjectives** come before **nouns**) and how they combine with other words (e.g. *a table*) because of grammar rules rather than because of lexical patterns such as **collocation**. It is not always easy to decide if a particular feature is categorised as grammatical or lexical. It is partly for this reason that we often refer to lexico-grammatical features.

Exercise 1

What lexical and grammatical features do the groups of words below show? If you need help with numbers 1 and 2, look at Unit 2; for number 3, look at Unit 4; for number 4 look at Unit 1.

1 big, tall, high
2 depart, bus, train
3 interested in doing something
4 go, going, went

Check your answers on page 119.

■ Parts of speech

All words are a grammatical **part of speech** (e.g. a noun, **verb**, adjective) and have a grammatical function in a sentence, i.e. they perform a grammatical role as a **subject**, an **object**, etc. (For more information on parts of speech and grammatical functions, see pages 51–2, Unit 10.)

Words can change their part of speech by changing their **form**. For example, *quick* is an adjective but *quickly* is an **adverb**; the change in form (adding the morpheme *ly*) has changed the part of speech. Sometimes, words can change their part of speech while keeping the same form. For example, in *I'm writing a book*, *writing* is functioning as a verb while in *his writing is hard to read*, it is functioning as a noun.

Suffixes and grammar

We saw in the previous section that we can make an adjective into an adverb by adding *ly*. In Unit 3 (see page 15) we looked at a range of **suffixes** that show different parts of speech. This use of suffixes is sometimes described as lexical and sometimes grammatical: lexical because the new word is an item of lexis (e.g. *teacher*); grammatical because the part of speech has changed or the suffix shows what part of speech the word is (e.g. *teach* is a verb, *teacher* is a noun).

Exercise 2

Underline the grammatical suffixes in the sentences below and decide what their grammatical functions are.

1 He works at a bank.
2 We walked to work yesterday.
3 You're laughing a lot!
4 She's taller than me.

Look at the table below to see if your answers were right.

Table 1 Grammatical suffixes

Grammatical suffixes	Functions	Examples
-s, -es, -en	Noun plurals	cats, dishes, children
-s	Third person singular **present simple tense** (regular)	he works, she lives
-ed	**Past simple tense** (regular)	we walked, I tried
-ing	Continuous **aspect, present participle, gerund**	you're laughing
-ed, -en	**Past participle**	I've wanted, we were beaten
-er, -est	**Comparative adjective, superlative adjective**	she's taller, he's the nicest

(based on *Cambridge Grammar of English* by Ronald Carter and Michael McCarthy, Cambridge University Press 2006)

Function words and lexis

Function words (sometimes called grammatical words) are words that do not have much lexical meaning but which have a grammatical function in a sentence. For example, the **auxiliary verb** *have* in *I have been a teacher for three years* has no lexical meaning: it is simply part of the **present perfect simple**. Function words contrast with **content words** (words that have their own lexical meaning) such as *teacher, three* or *years*. Some function words can also be used as content words. For example, *have* in *I have two brothers* is a content word because it has lexical meaning and is a main verb, not an auxiliary.

■ Grammar patterns and lexis

Exercise 3
Underline the mistakes in the sentences below.

1 On my opinion, this one is a best.
2 Can you advise me with the nicest place to stay?
3 We started of the beginning to September.
4 I'm grateful by the chance to help you.

Check your answers on page 119.

Something that may look like collocation occurs in many sentences but it can be more usefully described as a grammar pattern. For example, you might think that *the best* is a collocation because both words are very often seen together. However, collocation is the combination of items of lexis (nouns, verbs, adjectives and adverbs). *The* is not an item of lexis in this sense and is normally categorised as a function word. *The best* is an example of the grammar pattern in which *the* is used before superlative forms such as *best*.

We saw in Exercise 3 that certain prepositions combine with certain verbs, adjectives and nouns, and are used in certain phrases. We say *in my opinion* not *on my opinion*, *advise on* not *advise with* and *grateful for* not *grateful by*. Prepositions such as these are called **dependent prepositions** and their combination with verbs, nouns, etc. is often seen as a grammar pattern accompanying an item of lexis. A good English dictionary will tell you the prepositions that are most commonly used with different words.

Other verbs combine with adverb **particles**, and when they do they change their meaning. These are called **phrasal verbs**.

Exercise 4
There is a mistake in each of the sentences below. Correct the mistakes and then think about what changes you made to the sentences.

1 I really want trying Japanese food.
2 He offered taking me to the airport.
3 I'm interested in learn different languages.
4 She's tired of to wait for them arriving.

Check your answers on page 119.

You used your knowledge of grammar patterns with different items of lexis (verbs and adjectives) to correct the sentences above. The correct patterns tell us that the **infinitive form** (the base form of the verb with *to*) is used after certain verbs and the *-ing* form is used after certain adjectives, but this is not a general rule. For example, we can use the infinitive form after some adjectives (e.g. *happy to see you*) and the **-ing form** after some verbs (e.g. *I like living here*). For many items of lexis, a number of grammar patterns are possible and sometimes using one pattern rather than another can change the meaning. For example, we can say *he stopped talking* (he did not talk any more) and *he stopped to talk* (he stopped doing something and started talking). Table 2 shows grammar patterns with some common verbs and adjectives.

Table 2 Grammar patterns with some common verbs and adjectives

Verb or adjective	Example grammar patterns
want	+ infinitive form + object + infinitive form
give	+ indirect object + direct object + direct object + *to* + indirect object
agree	+ infinitive form + *that* + clause *to* + noun
suggest	+ *that* + clause + verb-*ing*
happy	+ *with* + noun + infinitive form
frightened	+ *of* + verb-*ing* (+ object) + *of* + noun

Some people use the term '*to* (+) infinitive' to make it clear that they are referring to the full infinitive form (e.g. *to go*).

A good dictionary will give the grammar patterns that go with items of lexis. For example:

> **want**   [+ **to** INFINITIVE]   What do you want to eat?
>
>   [+ OBJ + **to** INFINITIVE]   Do you want me to take you to the station?

(adapted from *Cambridge Advanced Learner's Dictionary (Third Edition)*,
Cambridge University Press 2008)

FOLLOW-UP ACTIVITIES   *(See page 119 for answers and commentary)*

1 Find the function words, content words and grammatical suffixes in the sentences below.
  1 I've been studying hard recently.
  2 I was asked to give a talk.
  3 They were going to school.

2 What grammar pattern follows the adjectives and verbs in the sentences below? Match the sentences with the grammar patterns.

Sentence	Grammar pattern
1 He was wrong _____ that to you.	a) *that* + subject + present simple
2 We're really pleased _____ winning.	b) + infinitive form
3 I suggest _____ .	c) + direct object + *from* + indirect object
4 Our umbrellas protected _____ the rain.	d) + *about* + verb-*ing*

DISCOVERY ACTIVITIES

1 Make a list of adjectives and verbs you have taught to your students recently. Are there any grammar patterns that follow these words? Are the grammar patterns that follow words included in the English language coursebooks you or your colleagues use?

2 Look at an authentic text (e.g. a newspaper article) and underline the grammar patterns that follow ten different words in the text. Write the grammar pattern (e.g. object + -*ing* form). Look in a good dictionary such as the *Cambridge Advanced Learner's Dictionary (Third Edition)*, Cambridge University Press 2008 to find other grammar patterns that follow these words.

TKT: KAL practice task 5 *(See page 133 for answers)*

A teacher is writing an information sheet on lexico-grammatical features for a teacher development session.

For questions **1-6**, match the example sentences with the features listed **A-G**.

There is one extra option which you do not need to use.

Lexico-grammatical features

A dependent preposition after a verb
B suffix showing a plural noun
C grammatical pattern following an adjective
D suffix showing a comparative
E verb with a grammatical function but no lexical meaning
F suffix showing the past simple
G suffix making a verb from a noun

Example sentences

1 The train finally stopped.
2 There were a thousand children at my school.
3 We were taken out to dinner by a friend.
4 Are you happier now?
5 I'm not very keen on visiting the museum.
6 He always worries about arriving too late.

Part 2 | Phonology

What is phonology?

Phonology is the study of how languages use **features** of sound to communicate meaning. In the English language, these features are often divided into five areas: **phonemes**, **word stress**, **sentence stress**, **intonation** and **connected speech**. The term 'pronunciation' is used to describe what happens when people use these different features in their speech. In the following four units we will look at each of these areas in turn.

Unit 6   Phonemes, and place and manner of articulation

■ Phonemes

A **phoneme** is the smallest unit of sound that has meaning in a language. For example, the sound /g/ in *got* is a phoneme in English because you can compare it with /h/ in *hot* and see that it gives the word a different meaning. There are 44 phonemes in the **variety of English** we refer to here.

> **Exercise 1**
> Look at the sentences below. How many phonemes are there in the underlined words? Which phoneme is different in the two words?
>
> 1 I <u>get</u> up early most days.
> 2 I <u>got</u> up early this morning.
>
> Now read the next section.

Both *get* /get/ and *got* /gɒt/ have three phonemes. Only the middle phoneme is different. When two words differ by only one phoneme, we call it a **minimal pair**. For example, *get* /get/ and *got* /gɒt/ are a minimal pair. /g/, /e/, /ɒ/, /t/ and /h/ are examples of **phonemic symbols** and each one represents a phoneme. When a word is written using phonemic symbols, it is called a **phonemic transcription**. For example, /gɒt/ is the phonemic transcription of *got*.

The 44 phonemic symbols of standard British English are often shown together in a **phonemic chart** like the one on page 30.

■ Phonemic chart

Vowels (sounds in which the air is not blocked by the tongue, lips, teeth, etc.)

Monophthongs				Diphthongs		
iː m<u>ee</u>t	ɪ s<u>i</u>t	ʊ l<u>oo</u>k	uː <u>you</u>	ɪə <u>ear</u>	eɪ s<u>ay</u>	
e t<u>e</u>n	ə <u>a</u>go	ɜː t<u>ur</u>n	ɔː s<u>aw</u>	ʊə p<u>ure</u>	ɔɪ b<u>oy</u>	əʊ n<u>o</u>
æ h<u>a</u>t	ʌ <u>u</u>p	ɑː <u>ar</u>m	ɒ h<u>o</u>t	eə <u>air</u>	aɪ f<u>i</u>ve	aʊ n<u>ow</u>

Consonants (sounds in which the air is partly blocked by the lips, tongue, teeth, etc.)

p <u>p</u>en	b <u>b</u>ad	t <u>t</u>en	d <u>d</u>o	tʃ <u>ch</u>in	dʒ <u>J</u>une	k <u>c</u>at	g <u>g</u>o
f <u>f</u>ive	v <u>v</u>an	θ <u>th</u>in	ð <u>th</u>en	s <u>s</u>o	z <u>z</u>oo	ʃ <u>sh</u>ip	ʒ plea<u>s</u>ure
m <u>m</u>an	n <u>n</u>ew	ŋ si<u>ng</u>	h <u>h</u>at	l <u>l</u>ate	r <u>r</u>ed	w <u>w</u>ill	j <u>y</u>es

(adapted from *Sound Foundations* by Adrian Underhill, Heinemann 1994)

Exercise 2

Using the phonemic chart above, write phonemic transcriptions of the following words: *looks, harm, bring, July, these.*

Check your answers and read the notes on page 120.

■ Long and short vowels

Exercise 3

Say the following words and decide if the vowel is long or short: *meet, sit, you, turn, saw, arm.* Look at the phonemic chart to see what the symbols for the long vowels have in common. Then read the next section.

In the phonemic chart, the symbol /ː/ means that a vowel sound is long. For example, the vowel sounds in *meet* and *sit* are similar except that the first is longer.

■ Vowels: place and manner of articulation

When you speak you can feel your tongue moving around your mouth, and your lips coming together and moving apart. This is how we make, or articulate, the different phonemes or sounds. The place of articulation of a phoneme is the place in your mouth where the phoneme is made. The manner of articulation is how a phoneme is made with the teeth, lips and other parts of the mouth. For example, sometimes your lips move together, sometimes they touch your teeth and so on.

Some phonemes are **voiced** and some are **unvoiced**. The term 'voiced phoneme' means that a sound is made by vibrating your voice, for example /ɑː/. You can feel this by putting your hand against your throat and saying /ɑː/. All vowel sounds are voiced. It is the manner and place of articulation which makes each vowel sound different.

Exercise 4

Say the phonemes below and decide where in your mouth they are made: towards the front, in the centre or at the back. For example, /iː/ is made towards the front of your mouth.

Try to feel what part of the mouth your tongue moves to in order to make each sound. For /iː/, your tongue is at the top of your mouth and towards the front.

/iː/ /ɪ/ /ʊ/ /uː/ /e/ /ə/ /ɜː/ /ɔː/ /æ/ /ʌ/ /ɑː/ /ɒ/

Check your answers on page 120.

It is not only the place of articulation that is important in producing a phoneme, it is also the manner.

Exercise 5

Say the pairs of vowel sounds below. What happens to your lips and mouth when you say them?

1 /iː/ /æ/   2 /uː/ /ɔː/   3 /iː/ /ɪ/.

Check your answers on page 120.

■ Diphthongs

Say the following words: *ear, boy, now*. All these words have vowel sounds that are made through a continuous movement from one vowel position to another. For example, in *ear*, from /ɪ/ to /ə/. In other words, they are made from two vowels. These are called **diphthongs**. Single vowel sounds, such as those in Exercise 4 and 5, are called monophthongs.

Exercise 6

Say the pairs of monophthongs below, making a continuous movement from one to the other.

/ʊ/ /ə/	/e/ /ɪ/	/e/ /ə/	/ɔː/ /ɪ/	/ə/ /ʊ/	/a/ /ɪ/	/ɪ/ /ə/	/a/ /ʊ/

Look at the phonemic chart on page 30 and decide which diphthong they make.

■ Consonants: manner and place of articulation

The parts of the mouth you use to make consonant phonemes are the teeth, the lips, the tongue, the top front of your mouth (the **alveolar ridge**), the top centre (the **palate**) and the top back (the velum). We use these parts of the mouth to make the air move from our mouths in different ways. For example, sometimes the air is stopped by putting the lips together and then it is suddenly released (a **plosive**) as in /b/ <u>buy</u>. The term 'plosive' refers to the manner of articulation. A sound which is made by bringing both lips together is a **bilabial** (*bi* – two, *labial* – lips). So, /b/ is a bilabial plosive. Bilabial refers to the place of articulation.

Some sounds are made by touching the tongue to the velum (the place of articulation). These are **velar** sounds (e.g. /k/). Sometimes air is released through the nose (a **nasal** sound) as in /n/ <u>nine</u>, and sometimes it is released between a small opening between the teeth or lips and the tongue, causing friction (a **fricative** sound) as in /f/ <u>fish</u>. If the sound is made by touching the lips and teeth together, it is called a **labio-dental**; /f/ is a labio-dental fricative.

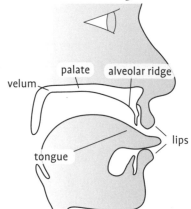

When air is blocked and then slowly released with friction, the phoneme is called an **affricate** as in /tʃ/ <u>church</u>. When air is released around the sides of the tongue, the phoneme is called a lateral as in /l/ <u>all</u>. Some consonant phonemes are voiced (e.g. /b/) and some are unvoiced (e.g. /p/).

Exercise 7

Look at the phonemic symbols below and say the consonant sounds they represent.

/f/   /n/   /tʃ/   /b/   /k/   /ð/   /l/

Match the phonemic symbols with the notes about the consonants in the table below. Write the correct phonemic symbol in the 'Consonant' column in the table.

Consonant	Notes
1	Air is blocked by putting the lips together. Then it is suddenly released. Voiced. Plosive.
2	Air is passed through a small opening between the top teeth and the bottom lip. Unvoiced. Fricative.
3	Air is passed through a small opening by putting the tongue between the teeth. Voiced. Fricative.
4	Air is blocked from the mouth with the tongue and passes through the nose instead. Voiced. Nasal.
5	Air is blocked by the tongue and then slowly released. Unvoiced. Affricate.
6	Air is blocked by pushing the tongue to the top back part of the mouth and then it is suddenly released. Unvoiced. Plosive.
7	Air is released around the sides of the tongue. Voiced. Lateral.

Check your answers on page 120.

When you say an unvoiced phoneme, it may sound as if it is voiced when it is followed by a vowel because the vowel phoneme is always voiced. Try saying /p/ and put your hand on your throat. You should feel no vibration because this phoneme is unvoiced. Now say /b/; you should feel vibration because this phoneme is voiced.

Look again at the phonemic chart on page 30 and find /p/ and /b/. You will see that in the first two lines of consonant sounds, the unvoiced and voiced sounds are in pairs, unvoiced on the left and voiced on the right. The phonemes in each pair are made in a very similar way but the difference is that one is unvoiced and one is voiced.

The table below gives the different types of consonant phoneme and their terms.

Manner of articulation	Examples
Plosive	/p/ /b/ /t/ /d/ /k/ /g/
Fricative	/f/ /v/ /θ/ /ð/ /s/ /ʃ/ /ʒ/ /z/ /h/ is normally called a fricative but you may see it called a pseudo-fricative.
Affricate	/tʃ/ and /dʒ/
Nasal	/m/ /n/ /ŋ/
Lateral	/l/

In English two or more consonant phonemes can occur together, either in a word or in two words that are spoken one after the other. This group of consonants is a **consonant cluster**. For example, in the word _crisps_ there is a consonant cluster at the end: /sps/; in _she likes football_ there is a consonant cluster between the second and third words: /ksf/.

The consonants /w/, /r/ and /j/ are often called semi-vowels. To make them, air passes through the mouth and nose with friction, as with all consonants. However, the friction is very little and this makes them more like vowels than consonants.

FOLLOW-UP ACTIVITIES _(See page 120 for answers)_

1 How many phonemes are there in each of the words below? What are they?
   Monday   student   difficult   flower

2 Match the underlined letters in the words below with the phonemic symbols.
   wh<u>y</u>   pl<u>ea</u>se   say<u>s</u>   g<u>ue</u>ss
   /e/   /iː/   /aɪ/   /z/

3 Write the words below using letters of the alphabet.
   /ˈverɪ/   /əˈnʌðə/   /ˈpiːpəl/   /tʃɪn/

4 Write the words below in phonemic script.
   secretary   sure   vegetable   playing

5 Say the consonant phonemes below and decide if they are plosive, fricative, affricate, nasal or lateral. Then decide if they are voiced or unvoiced.
   /t/   /dʒ/   /ŋ/   /s/   /v/

> ## DISCOVERY ACTIVITIES
>
> 1 Look at the phonemic chart on page 30. Which phonemes do you think your learners will have problems with? Why might they have problems with these phonemes?
> 2 Visit www.teachingenglish.org.uk/try/resources/pronunciation/phonemic-chart to practise phonemes and phonemic symbols, or have a look at the *Longman Pronunciation Dictionary (Third Edition)* by J. C. Wells, Pearson Education Ltd 2008, which has a CD with phonemes and other features of pronunciation.

TKT: KAL practice task 6 *(See page 133 for answers)*

A teacher is writing the answers to a quiz on phonemes to use in a development session for other teachers at her school.

For questions **1-6**, choose the correct answer **A**, **B** or **C**.

---

1 How many phonemes does the word *please* have?
  A two   **B** three   **C** four

2 Which of the following is a minimal pair?
  A so/soon   **B** me/tea   **C** thought/go

3 Which is the correct phonemic transcription for *Wednesday*?
  A /ˈwenzdeɪ/   **B** /ˈwensdeɪ/   **C** /ˈwednesdeɪ/

4 Which sound is a plosive?
  A /tʃ/   **B** /g/   **C** /θ/

5 In which sound do you need to open your mouth very wide?
  A /æ/   **B** /ɪ/   **C** /h/

6 Which phoneme is voiced?
  A /ʃ/   **B** /t/   **C** /z/

Unit 7 Stress patterns

LEARNING OUTCOME

KNOWLEDGE: how stress is used in words and sentences and why it occurs in particular places

■ Word stress

Words are made up of **syllables**; for example, *yesterday* has three syllables: *yes-ter-day*. The term **word stress** refers to the way that one of the syllables in a word is pronounced in a longer and louder way than the others. In *yesterday*, the first syllable is stressed: yes-ter-day. If a word has only one syllable, there is only one stress. For example, *big* has only one stress, which is placed on the **vowel**.

Exercise 1

Say the words below. How many syllables are there in each and which one is stressed? What is the word class of each word? Which words are compounds?

1 table   2 happy   3 decide   4 overtired   5 notebook   6 sociable   7 happily
8 organise   9 exercise   10 independently

Check your answers in the table below.

Examples	General rule about word stress
table happy	In many 2-syllable **nouns** and **adjectives**, the stress is on the first syllable.
decide	In many 2-syllable **verbs**, the stress is on the second syllable.
exercise sociable organise happily	In many 3-syllable nouns, adjectives, verbs and **adverbs**, the stress is on the first syllable.
notebook	In many **compound nouns** (two or more words used as a single noun), the stress is on the first word in the compound. It does not matter how many syllables there are in the compound as a whole, e.g. *skateboarding*.
overtired	In many compound adjectives, the stress is on the second word in the compound. It does not matter how many syllables there are in the word as a whole, e.g. *bad-tempered*. In this case, the first syllable of the second word is stressed because it is a 2-syllable word.
independently	In words with 4 or more syllables, the stress is normally somewhere in the middle of the word rather than at the beginning or the end.

Sometimes in English, words look as though they have more syllables than they actually do. For example, *sociable* looks as though it has four syllables (*so-ci-a-ble*) but it is normally pronounced with only three (*so-cia-ble*).

It is important to note that rules for word stress in English are general and there are always exceptions. Because of this, you should learn the stress in each word separately rather than depend completely on rules.

One way of finding the number of syllables in a word, and which is/are stressed, is to look in a good English dictionary where words are written in **phonemic transcriptions** and the stress is marked like this ', for example *family* /ˈfæmlɪ/.

■ Changing stress with word class

If you change the **word class** of a word, the stress pattern will often change. For example, some words can be both verbs or nouns and the word stress is different in each, e.g. *object* (verb), *object* (noun). Using **suffixes** also affects word stress, e.g. *photograph, photography*. Both these words are nouns but the suffix *-y* has moved the stress so that it follows the general rule for 4-syllable words in the table on page 35.

Exercise 2

Say the words below and decide where the stress is.

1 dependency   2 economic   3 biological   4 television   5 production

Check your answers and look at the table on page 120.

Suffixes are not generally stressed. For example, the common suffix *-ence* does not normally change the stress of the original word: *insist – insistence*.

Sometimes, words do not follow the general rules given in the table on page 35 because of the influence of a suffix. For example, *production* does not follow the general rule for 3-syllable nouns because of the influence of the suffix *-tion*.

■ Sentence stress: primary and secondary

In sentences some words are stressed more than others and there will always be a particular word in a sentence that has the **main stress** or the **primary stress**. For example, in the question *Are you happy?* the word *happy* is usually stressed. (This does not mean that all the syllables in that word are stressed – only the first syllable.) It is possible to say *Are you happy?* with stresses on different words but in its most common form *happy* has the primary stress. This is often referred to as the 'neutral' way of saying the sentence. We use the term 'neutral' to describe the sound of the sentence when there is no special effect given by the speaker. For example, the speaker does not want to sound angry or excited; it is just a simple sentence. In a neutral sentence, it is usually the last stressed syllable that receives the main **sentence stress**.

In the neutral sentence *I've lived here for five years* there are four stressed words: *lived, here, five* and *years*. These are the **content words** and they give the important information of the sentence. The word *five* is the most likely to have the primary stress because it is a content word and carries the main meaning of the sentence. The words *lived, here* and *years* have **secondary stress**, i.e. the stress is less strong than the primary stress.

In a neutral sentence, you can decide if a word has primary or secondary stress by changing the stresses. For example, in *I've lived here for five years* if you put the primary stress on *lived*, you change the emphasis and the sentence is no longer neutral; *lived* is emphasised for a particular effect. The other words in this sentence (*I've, for*) are grammatical words or **function words** (see page 25, Unit 5), which are unstressed because they are not generally essential for giving the important information.

Exercise 3

Underline the content words in the neutral sentences below. Which ones have the primary stress? Mark the stressed syllables in these words with a •.

1 Can you get the children? I'm still at work.
2 What's the best way to get to the station?

Check your answers on page 120 and look at the table below for examples of content and function words.

Content words: stressed	Function words: unstressed/weak
Main verbs	Auxiliary verbs
Nouns	Prepositions
Adjectives	Articles
Adverbs	Conjunctions
Negative auxiliaries	Pronouns

A good way to identify the content words (and therefore the stressed words) is to imagine receiving a brief text message. If you got a text message with *get children, still work*, you would probably understand it but if you received *can you the because I'm at*, you would not.

■ Weak forms in words and sentences

Unstressed words such as the function words *you* and *at* in number 1 in Exercise 3 contain a **weak form** (a vowel that is unstressed). The weak forms are /ɪ/, /ʌ/ and /ə/. The phoneme /ə/ is the most common weak form in English and is called a **schwa**.

Weak forms occur in sentences and in words as a result of 'forcing' syllables between the stressed words or syllables. For example, in English it should take you approximately the same amount of time to say *what's best way get sta-* as it takes to say *What's the best way to get to the station?*. The length of the unstressed words or syllables (*the, to, to the* and *-tion*) is reduced and the vowels become weak forms. Stressing some words or syllables and making others unstressed and weak is sometimes called the **rhythm** of a spoken sentence. It is a feature of **connected speech**. (For more information on connected speech, see page 45, Unit 9.)

Exercise 4

Say the sentences below neutrally and decide which words or syllables are weak.

1   I need to organise myself.
2   Can I take your photograph?
3   Have you got a notebook?
4   We had dinner and saw a film.
5   Do you like the shirt he bought?

Check your answers on page 120.

Longer individual words often have primary and secondary stress. For example, *organise* has only one weak syllable but this does not mean that both the other syllables have equal stress. As we saw on page 35, the first syllable is stressed in *organise*. This means that *-ise* is the secondary stress.

■ Contrastive stress in sentences

Exercise 5

Say the dialogue below. Where would you place the primary stress in B's sentences?

A: So, you've lived there for five years.
B: No, I've lived here for five years.
A: Oh! I thought you worked here.
B: No, I live here.

Now read the next section.

In B's first sentence, *here* has the primary stress and in B's second sentence the primary stress is on *live*. In both cases this is because B is correcting what A said. This is called **contrastive stress** and it often means changing the primary stress pattern from a neutral version. You use contrastive stress to show that information is significantly different from what has been said before: it contrasts with the information previously given.

■ Emphatic stress in sentences

Emphatic stress is similar to contrastive stress in that a word or syllable is stressed much more than would normally be the case. You use emphatic stress because you want to emphasise a particular point and give a particular piece of information extra importance. You are not necessarily *contrasting* it with a previously given piece of information or point. For example, in *John eats lots of ice cream. He* **loves** *it!*, *loves* has an emphatic stress because it is emphasising the strength of John's feelings. These feelings are not being contrasted with any others in this particular case.

Exercise 6

The words with a • above them in the sentences below have emphatic stress. What is the speaker trying to emphasise?

1 I've lived here for fi̊ve ye̊ars!
2 D̊o you like ice-cream?
3 I'm s̊o pleased to meet you!
4 H̊ow much did it cost?
5 I h̊ave to go now.

Check your answers on page 121.

In sentences with emphatic stress, you often find that function words can be stressed. For example, in sentence 2 above, the auxiliary *do* is stressed. This can also occur with contrastive stress. For example, A: *Did you drive in Paris?* B: *No, I drove **to** Paris.* When unstressed words become stressed, the weak forms become strong forms. For example, /tə/ becomes /tuː/.

FOLLOW-UP ACTIVITIES *(See page 121 for answers)*

1 How many syllables are there in the words below and which syllable is stressed? Do they follow any of the general rules?
greenhouse   believe   hotel   suddenly   photographic   point out   good-looking

2 Where is the primary stress in the neutral sentences below?
  1 I saw him yesterday.
  2 She's been to Paris.
  3 What time is it?

3 Underline the weak forms in the sentences in 2 and mark any that may be schwa /ə/.

4 Below are replies with contrastive stress. Write the questions. For example, reply:
No, he's the tall one. Question: *Is Tom the short man over there?*
  1 No, it's J̊ohn's. Mine is a Fiat.
  2 Actually, I h̊ate it.
  3 No, ȯn the table, please.

DISCOVERY ACTIVITIES

1 Listen to the radio or watch TV or DVDs and try to identify the stress patterns in the speakers' sentences. If you have subtitles, record part of a TV programme and copy the subtitles onto a piece of paper. Mark the stress on the subtitles and then play the programme with the sound. See if your stress patterns were right. Were emphatic or contrastive stress used?
2 Record your learners and find out what words they stress wrongly and/or whether they put the stress on function words rather than content words in sentences.

39

••

TKT: KAL practice task 7 *(See page 133 for answers)*

A teacher is giving feedback on her students' use of stress patterns in speaking.

For questions **1-6**, match the teacher's comments with the students' sentences listed **A-G**.

There is one extra option which you do not need to use.

Students' sentences

> **A** No, it's Mary who hates driving.
> **B** I work in administration.
> **C** I really like swimming.
> **D** They were speaking very quietly.
> **E** I like the present they gave me.
> **F** He doesn't like coffee.
> **G** What's your name?

Teacher's comments

1 You knew this word has the stress on the third syllable from the end. Well done.

2 Is the stress on the first or second syllable when this word is used as a noun rather than a verb?

3 You shouldn't stress the negative auxiliary so much in neutral sentences.

4 Good. You've got the primary stress just right in this neutral sentence.

5 It's good that you know this suffix means the stress is on the second syllable from the end.

6 Move the stress to the word after the one you've stressed; it'll add emphasis and show your meaning more clearly.

••

Unit 8 Intonation

LEARNING OUTCOME

KNOWLEDGE: how intonation varies depending on the type of sentence and the terms to describe intonation patterns

■ What is intonation?

Intonation is the term used to describe the way in which a person's voice moves up or down in order to give meaning to what they are saying. For example, in the question *How are you?*, the speaker's voice does not stay on one level but goes up and down on different parts of the question.

■ Pitch range and direction

Exercise 1

Say the sentences below in the way described in brackets. Does your voice start at a high level or a low one?

1 Where do you live? (normal, neutral question)
2 Good to see you! (pleased and excited)

Check your answers on page 121.

As we saw in Unit 7, we use the term 'neutral' to describe the sound of the question (or any other sentence) when there is no special effect given by the speaker; for example, the speaker does not want to sound angry or excited – it is just a simple question.

'Pitch' is the term used to describe the level of someone's voice when they are speaking, i.e. whether it is high or low. The difference between a speaker's highest pitch and lowest pitch is their pitch range. 'Pitch movement' describes the fact that pitch does not stay at a constant level when speaking: it moves. A movement in pitch is normally called 'tone' and we more commonly refer to tone movement than pitch movement. 'Pitch direction' is used to describe which direction the pitch (or tone) moves in.

Pitch movement can be in different directions. These are:

- Rise ↗ (your pitch goes up)
- Fall ↘ (your pitch goes down)
- Rise-fall ⌃ (your pitch goes up and then down)
- Fall-rise ⌄ (your pitch goes down and then up)

Intonation can be used to express the speaker's attitude, i.e. how they feel about something. In number 2 in Exercise 1, the speaker's pitch starts high on *Good*. It will normally then rise to *see* and then fall to *you*. The pattern across the whole sentence is a high fall; it is used to express excitement and pleasure.

There are no strict rules about which intonation pattern to use to express particular attitudes. However, there are some general connections which are given in Table 1.

Table 1 Attitudes and intonation patterns

Attitude	Intonation pattern
Irritation, anger	Low fall (though high fall is also possible)
Excitement, pleasure	High fall
Interest	High rise
Surprise	Middle fall-rise

■ Pitch direction and stress

Exercise 2

Decide where the primary stress is in the neutral sentence below. Then decide if the pitch changes from *I* to *help*.

Can I help you?

Now read the next section.

In the sentence above, the word *help* has the **primary stress**. The pitch rises from *I* to *help* (and then falls after *help*). In stressed words (**emphatic**, **contrastive**, primary or **secondary**), we not only make words louder and longer, but we also use a rising pitch.

■ Common intonation patterns

It is difficult to provide rules to describe when particular intonation patterns are used in English and there will always be exceptions. However, it is possible to provide very general rules that describe intonation in different types of sentence.

Exercise 3

Say the sentences below. Do you think the intonation rises or falls on the underlined words?

1 Are you <u>coming</u>?
2 Stop doing <u>that</u>!
3 She works at <u>home</u>.
4 What do you <u>want</u>?
5 This is yours, <u>isn't it</u>?
6 I've got <u>books</u>, a <u>pen</u>, a <u>pencil</u> and a <u>laptop</u>.

Check your answers in Table 2 on page 43.

Table 2 Sentence types and intonation patterns

Sentence type	Intonation pattern
1 Yes/No questions	Intonation often rises at the end but can also fall.
2 **Imperatives**	Intonation often falls at the end.
3 Statements	Intonation often falls at the end.
4 **Wh- questions**	Intonation often falls at the end.
5 **Question tags**	If you already know the answer, intonation often falls at the end. If you do not know the answer or are not sure, intonation often rises at the end.
6 Lists	Intonation often rises on each item in the list until the last one, where it falls.

In number 6 in Exercise 3, intonation is used partly to signal to the listener when to expect the list to continue and when to expect it to end. This is an example of how intonation can be used in **discourse** to help signal what information is coming next. For example, generally speaking, a listener knows that they should not interrupt after words with a rise because the speaker has not finished speaking. Similarly, when you hear a speaker's intonation fall at the end of a sentence, it is often a signal that it is your turn to speak. In this way, intonation is used to manage the interaction between speakers.

FOLLOW-UP ACTIVITIES   *(See page 121 for answers)*

1 Decide if the pitch at the beginning of the neutral sentences below is more likely to be high or low.
   1 What are you doing?   3 No, don't do that or I'll be angry.
   2 I'm so pleased for you!

2 Decide if the intonation at the end of the phrases below is more likely to rise or fall.
   1 Pass me the <u>salt</u>.   4 When did you get <u>here</u>?
   2 Look at that sun! Beautiful day, <u>isn't it</u>?   5 I bought milk, eggs and <u>bread</u>.
   3 Is this <u>yours</u>?

DISCOVERY ACTIVITIES

1 Record your learners to find out if they are effectively using intonation patterns to give their sentences the meaning they intend. Use this to create a lesson to help them with intonation.
2 Some published English-language courses have sections or even separate books and recordings that help students with pronunciation, including intonation. Look at a few coursebooks that you or your colleagues use. Is intonation practice included? What areas of intonation do they include? How useful is this for your students? (Alternatively, look at *New Headway Pronunciation Course: Intermediate Student's Practice Book*, by Bill Bowler *et al.*, Oxford University Press 2011 and answer the same questions.)

TKT: KAL practice task 8 *(See page 133 for answers)*

It is unlikely that a single task on intonation would be included in a TKT: KAL test. Items on intonation may be included as part of other tasks on phonology. For this reason, we have not included a full task in this unit. Below are two examples of items taken from a matching activity.

Match the students' phrases with the teacher's comments listed **A-B**.

Teacher's comments

> **A** Good. Your pitch moved up on this discourse marker.
> **B** Your intonation went up on the stressed words to show contrast. Well done.

Students' phrases

1 Apparently, the man we saw was …
2 No, not on the table, under it.

Unit 9   Connected speech

> **LEARNING OUTCOME**
>
> KNOWLEDGE: how pronunciation can change during connected speech and the terminology used to describe these changes

■ What is connected speech?

We use the term **connected speech** to refer to how pronunciation behaves and changes when you say phrases and sentences at natural speed to make a continuous stream of sound. In Unit 6 we looked at sounds in words spoken in isolation. In this unit we look at how these sounds often change when they occur in connected speech.

> **Exercise 1**
>
> Say the words *have* and *you*. Now say the sentence below at natural speed. How do the words *have* and *you* change?
>
> *Where have you been?*
>
> Now read the next section.

In a good dictionary, you will find two **phonemic transcriptions** of *have* (/hæv/ and /həv/ or /əv/) and of *you* (/juː/ and /jə/). The first transcription is the **strong form** and the second is the **weak form**. The weak form is common in connected speech in unstressed words but the strong form is used when the words are spoken in isolation.

■ Contractions

> **Exercise 2**
>
> Look at the dialogue below. What do you think happens to the underlined parts in connected speech?
>
> A: Hello! I <u>have</u> <u>not</u> seen you for ages! <u>Where</u> <u>have</u> you been?
> B: <u>I have</u> moved! <u>I am</u> living in Paris, with Sue.
> A: Really? How <u>long</u> <u>have</u> you been there?
> B: Um ... about five months.
> A: Have you got a nice flat?
> B: <u>It is</u> OK. <u>It is</u> <u>not</u> very big but <u>it is</u> in a nice area.
>
> Check your answers on page 121.

The term **contraction** refers to the way some words join together and parts of words, often **auxiliary verbs**, are left out when groups of words are said at a natural speed. For example, *I have* often becomes *I've* /aɪv/ because the /hæ/ has been left out. Some words can contract in different ways, for example *it is not* can be *it's not* /ɪts nɒt/ or *it isn't* /ɪt ɪzənt/.

When you use contractions in writing, it often means that the **register** or **style** is **informal**. In speech it is very normal to use contractions whether the register is **formal** or informal. When a speaker chooses not to use contractions in speech, it is often because they want to **emphasise** or draw attention to a particular word. For example, in *I am living in Paris*, the word *am* will not be contracted if the speaker wants to disagree with someone who said *I know you aren't living in Paris*. In this case, *am* will also be stressed (as an **emphatic** stress, as described on pages 38–9 in Unit 7).

■ Linking

Another feature of connected speech is **linking**, in which the final sound of a word continues into the next word. For example, in *got a nice flat* the final sound /t/ of *got* links to the sound /ə/ of *a*. The phonemic transcription of this would be /gotə naɪs flæt/. Linking such as this happens at **word boundaries**, i.e. the place where one word ends and another begins. Linking such as this often happens when a **consonant** sound precedes a **vowel** sound. However, speakers do not always link consonants to vowels. For example, when being emphatic, you might say each word separately without consonant–vowel linking.

Exercise 3

Say the dialogue below at natural speed and mark the consonant–vowel linking like this:
I'm living͜ in Paris.

A: Can you recommend a good hotel in Paris?
B: Um, not really. You should ask Sue. She'd know.
A: OK, thanks. I'll ask her.
B: She's away at the moment, but she'll be back on Tuesday.

Check your answers on page 122.

■ Intrusion

Sometimes words are linked in connected speech by adding another sound between them. For example, if you say the words *he ate* at natural speed, you will hear a /j/ sound appear between *he* and *ate*: /hiːjeɪt/.

Exercise 4

Say the dialogue below at natural speed and decide what sound links the words in the places underlined.

A: Where's she gone?
B: India and China. She asked me to go with her. But I had to ask my boss and he said no.

Check your answers on page 122.

In these sentences, the sounds /r/, /j/ and /w/ are called **intrusive**. Like consonant–vowel linking, intrusive sounds join words in connected speech but they are used to join vowel sounds. The sounds are created as you move from one vowel to the next.

The table below shows when these intrusive sounds are likely to be produced.

Intrusive sound	When it is likely to be produced	Examples
/w/	Between words ending in /uː/, /əʊ/ and /aʊ/ and words beginning with a vowel sound.	to ask /tuːwɑːsk/ No, I'm not /nəʊwaɪm/ How are you? /haʊwɑː/
/j/	Between words ending in /iː/, /ɪ/, /eɪ/, /ɔɪ/ and /aɪ/ and words beginning with a vowel sound.	A <u>tree in</u> a park /triːjɪn/. When did <u>he arrive</u>? /hiːjəraɪv/ (Note: *he* could be strong or weak here: /hiː/ or /hi/. The linking remains the same.) A <u>day in</u> August /deɪjɪn/. A <u>boy and</u> his friend /bɔɪjən/ I <u>asked</u> you a question /aɪjɑːskt/
/r/	Between words ending in /ə/ and /ɔː/ and words beginning with a vowel sound.	<u>India and</u> China /ɪndɪərən/ <u>More and</u> more /mɔːrən/

Note that although in British English the /r/ in the phrase *the teacher and me* is considered intrusive, in North American English this is consonant–vowel linking as the /r/ in *teacher* is pronounced (/ˈtiːtʃər/) in this variety of English.

Intrusion can also happen between the **syllables** of a word. For example, in the word *going* there is an intrusive /w/ between *go* and *ing*: /ˈgəʊwɪŋ/.

■ Assimilation

In natural speech, some sounds can change because of the effect of the sound next to them. This is called **assimilation**. For example, in *a piece of green paper* the sound /n/ at the end of *green* can change to /m/ because it is followed by a /p/. This is because the speaker is bringing their lips together to make the sound /p/ while finishing the word *green*. In the sentence *Tom is coming*, the **voiced sound** /z/ in *is* can change to the **unvoiced sound** /s/. This is because the following sound /k/ is unvoiced. It is easier for the speaker to make both sounds unvoiced.

The influence of voiced/unvoiced sounds can help us predict the pronunciation of some words. For example, in regular verbs, if the **infinitive form** of the verb ends in a voiced sound, the *-ed* ending is likely to be pronounced /d/ – another voiced sound. For example, the /n/ in *open* is voiced, so the *-ed* in *opened* is pronounced /d/. If the infinitive form of the verb ends in an unvoiced sound, the *-ed* ending is likely to be pronounced /t/ – another unvoiced sound. For example, the /k/ in *ask* and the /ʃ/ in *finish* are unvoiced, so the *-ed* in *asked* and *finished* is pronounced /t/. Note, however, when the infinitive form of the verb ends in *t* or *d*, and the **past simple** form ends with *-ted* or *-ded* (e.g. *wanted*, *depended*), the *-ed* is likely to be pronounced /ɪd/.

> ### Exercise 5
> Say the dialogue below at natural speed. How can the underlined sounds change?
>
> B: I'm sorry. I really ha<u>v</u>e to go!
> A: OK. Is thi<u>s</u> your handbag?
> B: Yes, thanks. I mustn't forget that!
> A: And coul<u>d y</u>ou pass me the brow<u>n</u> bag? It's mine.
> B: Sure. Here you are.
>
> Check your answers on page 122.

■ Elision

The term **elision** is used to describe the way that some sounds that are in a word when it is spoken on its own disappear when it is used in connected speech. For example, in *I don't know*, the sound /t/ in *don't* may not be pronounced: /dənəʊ/.

> ### Exercise 6
> Say the extract from the dialogue below at natural speed. Which sounds are elided (omitted)?
>
> A: OK. Is this your handbag?
> B: Yes, thanks. I mustn't forget that!
>
> Check your answers on page 122.

It is consonant sounds that are elided and the most common consonants to be elided are /t/ and /d/. Sometimes, /t/ and other plosive sounds made at the back of the throat are not elided but are not completely pronounced either. For example, the /t/ in *forget* is often 'stopped' before it is completely pronounced. We call this a **glottal (stop)** sound and it is represented by a /ʔ/ symbol.

Of course, speakers do not have to assimilate or elide sounds when they speak but if they do not, it often means they are adding extra meaning to what they say. For example, a speaker saying *I don't know* with no elision will sound emphatic, perhaps irritated.

FOLLOW-UP ACTIVITIES *(See page 122 for answers)*

1 Look at the transcription of a sentence in English below. Some of the words are written together to show features of connected speech. Write the sentence in letters (i.e. *I've been …*) and label the different features of connected speech.

/aɪv bɪn stʌdjɪŋɪŋglɪʃ fə temʌnθzənɪts nɪəlɪ ðiːjendəv ðə kɔːs/

2 Say the phrases below at natural speed. Use phonemic script to write the underlined parts.
   1 <u>You and</u> me.
   2 <u>Hi, I'm</u> John.
   3 <u>Did you live in</u> town?
   4 <u>Is she</u> still <u>in bed</u>?

1 List some words whose pronunciation you have taught your students recently. Put the words into sentences and decide if their pronunciation changes because of connected speech.

2 Look at a book about pronunciation such as the *Longman Pronunciation Dictionary (Third Edition)* by J. C. Wells, Pearson Education Ltd 2008, or *New Headway Pronunciation Course: Intermediate Student's Practice Book* by Bill Bowler *et al.*, Oxford University Press 2011, which have CDs with features of connected speech. Which features described in this unit are in these books?

TKT: KAL practice task 9 *(See page 133 for answers)*

A teacher has written a quiz on features of connected speech to use in a teacher development session.

For questions **1-7**, match the underlined examples of features of connected speech with the quiz answers listed **A-D**.

You will need to use some options more than once.

Quiz answers

> **A** elision
> **B** assimilation
> **C** intrusion
> **D** consonant–vowel linking

Examples of features of connected speech

1 I <u>live in</u> /lɪvɪn/ the south
2 <u>No, I'm</u> /nəʊwaɪm/ not
3 There were <u>ten boys</u> /tembɔɪz/.
4 See you <u>next time</u> /nekstaɪm/.
5 Are you from <u>America or</u> /əmerɪkərɔː/ Canada?
6 I'm going abroad <u>this year.</u> /ðɪʃɪə/.
7 Do you <u>want an apple</u> /wɒntənæpəl/?

What is grammar?

Grammar is how we organise words in phrases and sentences and how we change the form of words to give meaning to what we say or write. An English sentence uses two areas of grammar: the order of words (**syntax**) and how individual words are structured or made (morphology). Syntax and morphology work together to give sentences meaning.

Unit 10   Syntax and morphology

■ Syntax

The meaning of *bought her she birthday presents lots of* is difficult to understand because of the word order. We need to reorder the words to make a sentence that has meaning. The rules of **syntax** mean that there is normally only one way to order these words in this sentence: *She bought her lots of birthday presents.*

Exercise 1

Look at the sentence above again. Match the words as they are used in it with the labels a)–d).

1	She	a)	verb
2	bought	b)	subject
3	her	c)	indirect object
4	birthday presents	d)	direct object

Write down some rules of syntax about the order of these words in the sentence. For example: A subject (*she*) normally comes before a verb (*bought*) in this type of sentence.

Check your answers on page 122.

It is our knowledge of syntax that allows us to understand the relationship between words in a sentence and to order them according to the rules.

■ Morphology

In the word *presents*, as it is used in the example sentence in the previous section, the *s* at the end of the word shows us it is a regular plural **noun**. In the word *bought*, the combination of letters tells us this **verb** is in the past. It is different from *buys*. Knowledge of morphology helps us understand that a word is plural, or is in the past, or is a **subject**, an **object**, an **adverb** and so on. One reason you could understand *bought her she birthday presents lots of* in the previous section was because the morphology was correct; all you needed to do was reorder the words. However, if the morphology and syntax are seriously incorrect, the meaning becomes very difficult to understand, as in *buyed hers her birthdays present lots of*.

■ Parts of speech / word classes

Part of speech or **word class** are the labels we use to describe a word's grammatical function or the grammatical group to which it belongs. In the sentence *She bought her lots of birthday presents*, the word *She* is a subject pronoun. A **pronoun** is a part of speech that replaces a noun and refers to a person or a thing. There are nine parts of speech in English: nouns, verbs, **adjectives**, adverbs, **determiners**, **prepositions**, pronouns, **conjunctions** and exclamations.

Exercise 2

Look at the sentence below. There are two words beginning with *wonder*. What parts of speech are these two words?

She bought her lots of wonderful birthday presents: a wonderfully funny book and ...

Now read the next section.

A change to the **form** of a word can change the word's part of speech. In the sentence above, the adjective *wonderful* becomes the adverb *wonderfully* with the addition of the **morpheme** *ly*. This is called **affixation**: the addition of small units at the beginning, at the end or within words to change their meaning or part of speech. For example, *possible – **im**possible* (the meaning is changed by adding a **prefix**) and *snow – snow**y*** (the noun becomes an adjective by the addition of a **suffix**). (For more information on affixation, see Units 3 and 5.)

Exercise 3

Look at the two sentences below. What part of speech is *spoken* in each sentence?

1   I've spoken English for years.
2   Spoken English is sometimes hard to understand.

Check your answers on page 122.

Sometimes, the form of a word remains the same but the part of speech changes because the function of the word changes. To help you decide what part of speech a word is, you need to consider the following:

- its function in the sentence
- its form (morphology)
- its position in the sentence (syntax).

You can also find out what part of speech a word is, how it can change its form, how it can be used in terms of word order, its meaning/use and example sentences by looking in a good dictionary.

Exercise 4

Look at the dialogue below and decide what parts of speech the underlined words are.

On the phone

Suzi: Hello?
Jan: Suzi? Hi! It's Jan.
Suzi: Hey … how are you? How was your party?
Jan: Really good actually … sorry you couldn't come.
Suzi: … and I'm sorry, too, really sorry … kids, school … you understand, don't you?
Jan: Totally … no problem. You were missed. Thanks for the lovely present.
Suzi: Was it at home when you arrived? Have you tried it?
Jan: Absolutely … I used it for the first time yesterday, but I'm not very good at it!

Check your answers in the table below.

Part of speech	How it functions	Examples
Adjective	Describes and gives more information about a noun, **noun phrase** or pronoun.	*good, better* (comparative), *best* (superlative), *lovely*
Adverb	Gives more information about adjectives, adverbs, verbs, or whole **phrases** and sentences, e.g. by saying when or where something happens.	*totally* (degree), *yesterday* (time), *quickly* (manner)
Conjunction	Connects words, **clauses** or sentences and shows how they relate to each other.	*but* (contrast), *and* (addition), *when* (time)
Determiner	Tells you which noun is being referred to or tells you about quantity.	*your* (possessive), *the* (definite article)
Exclamation	Shows a feeling and is usually **informal**.	*Hi!* (friendly greeting), *Er …* (doubt)
Noun	Gives the name of things, people, places, etc.	*party, kid* (countable nouns), *London* (proper noun)
Preposition	Connects a noun, noun phrase or pronoun to other words or phrases and shows how they relate to each other.	*at* (place), *towards* (direction), *before* (time)
Pronoun	Replaces a noun or noun phrase.	*you* (personal, subject pronoun), *mine* (possessive pronoun)
Verb	Shows an action or state.	*could* (modal), *do* (auxiliary), *arrived* (intransitive), *have* (auxiliary)

For more information on the parts of speech above, go to:

- Unit 11 (nouns, determiners, adjectives)
- Units 12 and 13 (verbs)
- Unit 12 (adverbs)
- Unit 14 (conjunctions).

FOLLOW-UP ACTIVITIES *(See pages 122–3 for answers)*

1 Read the sentences below and decide what parts of speech the underlined words are. Include other information you know about each underlined word, e.g. *told* is past simple, irregular.
   1 He told me the problem yesterday.
   2 We should have arrived at the cinema earlier.
   3 She was very tired but completely happy.
   4 Is this your book or is it mine? I'm really not sure.
   5 Be careful! That water's boiling! Put it down!

2 Which part of speech is each of the words below? To help you, think of the words in sentences. Some words can be more than one part of speech.

1	go	7	drive
2	written	8	ouch
3	myself	9	whereas
4	so	10	when
5	almost	11	best
6	like	12	all

DISCOVERY ACTIVITY

1 Use two of these grammar references to look up some of the words in the Follow-up activities. Which one is more useful for finding out about parts of speech? Why?
   Cambridge Advanced Learner's Dictionary (Third Edition), Cambridge University Press 2008
   English Grammar in Use (Third Edition) by Raymond Murphy, Cambridge University Press 2004
   Uncovering Grammar by Scott Thornbury, Macmillan 2001
   http://learnenglish.britishcouncil.org/en/quick-grammar

∙∙

TKT: KAL practice task 10 *(See page 133 for answers)*

A trainer is using an email she has received as part of a teacher development session on parts of speech and is writing the answer key.

For questions **1-6**, complete the answer key by choosing the line in the email (**A**, **B** or **C**) which contains an example, or examples, of the parts of speech.

Email

Hi Katy!	
Hope it's going well with you. It's great here. Really having	*line 1*
the best time in Rome. The food is great, Italian people are	*line 2*
so friendly and the weather is fantastic. I wish you were here	*line 3*
with me. I've been really busy every day so far and, because	*line 4*
I'm working hard, my Italian is improving at the moment. Do	*line 5*
you think you'll be able to get over to visit before I come	*line 6*
back next month? Let me know when you can.	*line 7*
Hope to see you as soon as possible.	*line 8*
John xxx	

Example(s) of parts of speech

1 subject pronoun
   A line 2   **B** line 5   **C** line 8
2 conjunction of addition
   A line 2   **B** line 3   **C** line 5
3 preposition of place
   A line 2   **B** line 5   **C** line 8
4 proper noun
   A line 1   **B** line 5   **C** line 6
5 adjective
   A line 4   **B** line 5   **C** line 8
6 adverb of manner
   A line 2   **B** line 3   **C** line 5

∙∙

Unit 11 The noun phrase and adjectives

LEARNING OUTCOME

KNOWLEDGE: the structure of noun phrases, the use of adjectives, and key terms associated with noun phrases

■ What is a noun phrase?

A **noun phrase** is a group of words or a single word that acts as a **noun** in a **phrase** or sentence. For example, *my best friend* is a noun phrase. It could be followed by a **verb phrase**, for example *arrived early at the party*. In this case, *the party* is another noun phrase. A noun phrase can be one word (e.g. *John, she, people*) or it can be longer, as in the examples above. Sometimes, a noun phrase can be more complicated, for example the underlined part of *The woman who answered the door was very friendly*.

■ Different types of noun

> ### Exercise 1
> Look at the sentences below and decide what type of noun each underlined noun is. Some of the nouns have more than one term to describe them. For example, *city* is a common, countable noun.
>
> 1 London is a city in the UK.
> 2 The staff here thinks money is important.
> 3 I can see the pleasure your family gives you.
>
> Read the table below to check your answers.

Type of noun	Notes	Examples
Proper noun	Often the names of specific places, people and organisations; begin with a capital letter.	London, John, the Government, the UK, Mount Everest
Common noun	Non-specific things, e.g. there are lots of *cities* in the world.	city, money, family, people, dogs, cats
Countable noun	Can be singular or plural; you can have a number of them.	city, family, men, (an) apple, (three) apples
Uncountable noun	Cannot have a plural form; you cannot have a number of them, e.g. *I've got two informations* (✗).	money, pleasure, freedom, information, air, water, rice
Collective noun	Generally used for a group of things, people, animals and places.	(the) staff, family, (the) army, furniture, team
Concrete noun	Used for real, physical things that you can touch, see, taste, etc.	city, money, family, John, Mount Everest, London, staff
Abstract noun	Used for non-physical things that you can't touch, see, taste, etc.	pleasure, freedom, information, love, power

Some nouns, called **compound nouns**, are made of more than one word. For example, *bus stop* is a common, concrete, countable noun made from a noun + a noun. We can form nouns from other **parts of speech** by adding **suffixes**: for example, by adding the suffix -*ment* to the verb *advertise* we form the noun *advertisement* (see Unit 3 and Unit 10). The process of making nouns from other parts of speech is called nominalisation. Nominalisation occurs most commonly with verbs and adjectives. We can also form nouns by adding -*ing* to a **verb** (e.g. *I like swimming*). When a verb with an -*ing* ending is used as a noun, it is called a **gerund**.

Exercise 2

Look at the words and write their noun forms. (Do not use gerunds for the verbs.)

1 happy (adjective) _____
2 long (adjective) _____
3 revise (verb) _____
4 fly (verb) _____

Now read the next section.

Some common suffixes used in nominalisation are: -*ness* (*happiness*), -*tion* (*production*), -*ion* (*revision*), -*ment* (*advertisement*), -*ance* (*reliance*), -*ence* (*dependence*). Other forms used for nominalisation appear to be more irregular but there are still patterns. For example: *long – length, strong – strength, deep – depth, wide – width, fly – flight, high – height, see – sight, live – life, believe – belief, relieve – relief*.

Some verbs can also be used as nouns with no changes to their form. For example, *love*, which is a verb and an abstract noun. In this case, the meaning does not change greatly. *I love him* means 'I have feelings of great affection for him'; *Love is important* means 'The feeling of great affection is important'.

■ Determiners

Determiners are words that usually come at the beginning of a noun phrase and tell us something more about the noun and help to **qualify** (define or identify) it. For example, in the sentence *this is my coat*, the word *my* is a determiner. It identifies the coat as the one that belongs to me.

Exercise 3

Look at the underlined determiners in the sentences below and decide what information they give about the noun or how they identify it. For example, *the* = a specific car, a car we already know about.

1 Is that <u>the</u> car you want to buy?
2 Do you want <u>this</u> book or <u>that</u> one?
3 I've got <u>two</u> brothers but <u>no</u> sisters.
4 I don't buy <u>many</u> new clothes because I don't have <u>much</u> money.
5 <u>Both</u> my brothers work in the city but <u>neither</u> is happy.
6 There isn't really <u>enough</u> time to discuss <u>all</u> the possibilities.

Read the table on the next page to check your answers.

Type of determiner	Notes	Examples
Article	Used to identify a specific noun, e.g. one we already know about (definite article), or a non-specific noun (indefinite article). There are many rules for using articles that you will be able to find in a good English grammar.	*the* car (definite article), *a* car (indefinite article), *cars* (zero article)
Possessive adjective	Used to identify who possesses or owns the noun.	*my* coat, *your* coat, *his, her, its, our, their*
Demonstrative adjective	Used to identify how close or distant the noun is to the speaker.	*this* book / *these* books (generally near), *that* book / *those* books (generally distant)
Quantifier	Used to identify how much or how many of something, how complete something is or if something is sufficient. Some quantifiers are used with either countable or uncountable nouns. For example, *many* (countable) and *much* (uncountable). Some are used with both countable or uncountable nouns (e.g. *no sisters, no sugar*). Quantifiers may be made of more than one word (e.g. *a lot of*). There are a number of other examples of quantifiers that you will be able to find in a good English grammar.	*two* brothers / *no* sisters (number) *many* clothes / *much* money (number or amount) *no* sisters / *no* sugar (number and amount) *both* brothers / *neither* brother (number) *enough* time (sufficient) *all* (completeness)

■ Modifiers

Modifiers are used to define, describe or identify a noun but, unlike determiners, they can be placed before or after the noun.

Exercise 4
Describe the underlined modifiers below.

1 an <u>oil</u> painting

2 an <u>old</u> oil painting

3 an old oil painting <u>of his house</u>

4 my <u>friend's</u> old oil painting of his house

Check your answers on page 123.

There are various ways of modifying nouns. These include using nouns placed before the noun they modify (e.g. *oil* – see compounds in Unit 3), **adjectives**, which are also often placed before the noun (e.g. *old*), **possessive 's'** (e.g. *friend's*), and prepositional phrases, which are placed after the noun they modify (e.g. *of his house*). More **complex** clauses can also modify nouns. For example, in *a picture that he's had for years*, the underlined part is a **relative clause** (see page 77, Unit 14) which modifies *picture*. Relative clauses are placed after, and as close as possible to, the noun they modify.

■ Adjectives

In Exercise 4, the adjective *old* was used to modify (describe) the noun *oil painting*. Using adjectives is an extremely common way of modifying a noun or noun phrase.

Exercise 5

Write the adjectives formed from the words below.

1 act (verb) _____
2 use (verb) _____
3 nerve (noun) _____

4 rain (noun) _____
5 amuse (verb) _____
6 write (verb) _____

Check your answers on page 123.

Adjectives can be formed from verbs and nouns by adding suffixes (e.g. *useful, rainy*) and by using the **present participle** and **past participle** forms (e.g. *amusing, written*). Adjectives can also be made by combining two words (e.g. *homesick*: a noun + an adjective). (For more information on **affixation** used in adjectives, see page 15, Unit 3.)

In a noun phrase, adjectives are normally placed before the noun (e.g. *a very happy man*). Some adjectives can *only* come after the noun (e.g. *asleep, awake*). When there are two or more adjectives in a noun phrase, the patterns in the table below might be followed.

Size	*Shape*	*Colour*	*Origin*	*Material*	*Use*	*Noun*
huge		white				buildings
	round	blue		metal		discs
			American		running	shoes

(based on *Grammar for English Language Teachers* by Martin Parrott, Cambridge University Press 2000, 2010)

Exercise 6

Complete the sentences below with an appropriate adjective in the correct form.

1 I've seen many good films, but this one is the _____ .
2 He's 172 cm tall, and I'm 180, so I'm _____ than him.
3 I'm intelligent, John's _____ intelligent than me but Jo's the _____ intelligent of all of us.

What changes did you make to the adjectives *good*, *tall* and *intelligent*?

Check your answers on page 123.

Comparative adjectives are used when comparing two things; **superlative adjectives** are used when comparing more than two things. Comparative adjectives are made by adding either *-er* to the adjective or putting *more* before the adjective. Superlative adjectives are formed by adding *-est* to the adjective or putting *the most* before the adjective. You usually add *-er/-est* when an adjective has one or two syllables (e.g. *smaller/smallest, simpler/simplest*) and you usually add *more/the most* when it has two, three or more syllables (e.g. *more simple / the most simple, more expensive / the most expensive, more intelligent / the most intelligent*). In the case of irregular comparatives and superlatives, the form of the adjective itself changes (e.g. *good – better – best*). (For more information on comparative and superlative forms, refer to a good grammar reference.)

Some adjectives are **gradable** (they can be measured in degrees). For example, you can be more or less *cold*. Some adjectives are **ungradable** (they cannot be measured in degrees). For example, something cannot be more than *freezing*. For this reason, ungradable adjectives do not normally have comparative and superlative forms.

With gradable adjectives, we use **intensifiers** (**adverbs** that make the meaning of another word stronger) that describe the degree of cold, heat, etc. that something is. For example, we can say something is *very cold, extremely cold, quite cold, a little cold*. With ungradable adjectives, we use intensifiers that emphasise their extreme quality. For example, we can say *absolutely/completely/totally freezing*. You can use intensifiers with both kinds of adjective (e.g. *very cold, absolutely freezing*) but, often, you cannot use them interchangeably, e.g. *absolutely cold* (✗).

FOLLOW-UP ACTIVITIES *(See page 123 for answers)*

1 Label the main nouns, determiners and modifiers in the underlined noun phrases below. For example, in *This is my old car*, *my* is a determiner (possessive), *old* is an adjective, *car* is a common noun.
   1 I live in a large white house by the sea.
   2 Dave bought me some lovely Spanish jewellery for my birthday.
   3 Why do you want the cheap, green one?

2 Identify and describe each of the adjectives in the sentences below. Say, for example, how it is made and where it is placed in the sentence. For example, in *a boring book*, the adjective is *boring*, it is a present participle, made from verb + *-ing*, and is placed immediately before the noun.
   1 She gave a very lengthy speech.
   2 I'm feeling completely exhausted at the moment.
   3 He really hates stormy weather.
   4 They're happier than they used to be.

DISCOVERY ACTIVITY

1 Find a short article in a newspaper or magazine (film or book reviews are good for this purpose) and look at a couple of sentences.
   Circle the nouns in the sentences and then label them *proper, common, countable, uncountable, collective, concrete* or *abstract*.
   Underline the noun phrases in the sentences and then identify the determiners, modifiers, prepositional phrases, etc.

· ·

TKT: KAL practice task 11 *(See page 133 for answers)*

A teacher is writing some notes to help her plan a training workshop for her colleagues focusing on noun phrases and adjectives.

For questions **1-6**, match the teacher's notes with the underlined examples of noun phrases and adjectives listed **A-G**.

There is one extra option which you do not need to use.

Examples

> **A** What <u>a huge dog</u>!
> **B** He gave me <u>two books</u>.
> **C** The weather <u>is getting colder</u>.
> **D** Is she the <u>girl who plays guitar</u>?
> **E** Do you mean <u>the car</u> outside the house?
> **F** <u>This is yours</u>, isn't it?
> **G** Do you have <u>much money</u>?

Teacher's notes

1 This quantifier comes before a plural countable noun.
2 The adjective comes after this verb and so it's also after the subject of the sentence.
3 The relative clause comes after the noun.
4 The definite article means you've mentioned the noun before.
5 Use this quantifier with uncountable nouns.
6 The adjective comes before the noun.

· ·

Unit 12   The verb phrase and adverbs

LEARNING OUTCOME

KNOWLEDGE: how verb phrases are formed, and different verb patterns and their meanings

■ What is a verb phrase?

A **verb phrase** is the part of the sentence that contains the **verb** or verbs. For example, the underlined part of *I want to learn Japanese* is a verb phrase. Verb phrases can be: single verbs (e.g. *think*); **multiword verbs** (e.g. *grow up*); **auxiliary verbs** and the main verb (e.g. *have/has been working*); or two main verbs (e.g. *want to learn*, *stop speaking*). You can also find verb phrases within **noun phrases** (see Unit 11). For example, *the people who want to learn Japanese*.

■ Different types of verb

Exercise 1

Use the different types of verbs in the box to label the underlined verbs in the sentences. For example, in number 1 *Do* is an auxiliary verb. Some verbs can be matched with more than one type.

main	auxiliary	action	state	transitive	intransitive	reflexive

1 Do I know you?   3 I was talking.
2 He hurt himself.   4 They didn't see me.

Check your answers on page 124 and then read the table below and on page 62.

Type of verb	Notes about meaning and form	Examples
Main	• They have lexical meaning (unlike auxiliary verbs). • They have different forms (e.g. *knows, knowing, knew*). • They can combine with auxiliary verbs (e.g. *Do I know you?*).	*know, believe, talk, see, go, dress*
Auxiliary	• They are used in forming **tenses** (e.g. *he has gone*), questions (e.g. *Do I know you?*) and negatives (e.g. *They didn't see me*) and the **passive voice** (e.g. *I was seen*).(See Unit 13.) • They are not used in neutral positive **present** and **past simple tenses** (e.g. *I know, I knew*) except when modal. • They can also be used to replace the main verb (e.g. *I know but nobody else does*). (See Unit 16.) • *Have, do* and *be* can also act as main verbs (e.g. *Can I have a shower?* vs. *I have visited them, I do my homework every evening* vs. *Do you like school?, I'm a teacher* vs. *I'm going to school*).	All forms of *be, have* and *do* can be used as auxiliaries. **Modal verbs**, e.g. *can, could, may.*

Type of verb	Notes about meaning and form	Examples
Action	• These are also sometimes called 'event' verbs or **dynamic verbs**. • These are main verbs that describe an action. • They can be used in a continuous form (e.g. *talking*).	*talk, see, go, eat, break, dress*
State	• These are also sometimes called **stative** verbs. • These are main verbs that describe a condition or state. • Often, they cannot be used in a continuous form though some can when they are used as action verbs (e.g. *I was <u>having</u>* (event) *a shower* vs. *I <u>have</u>* (condition/state) *two brothers*). • When state verbs are used as action verbs, they change their meaning, e.g. *having* = the act of taking a shower, not 'possessing' a shower.	*know, believe, belong, smell, have*
Transitive	• Verbs that need an object in order to make sense, e.g. we cannot say *I love*, it needs an object: *I love you*. • Some verbs can take two objects (e.g. *give: I gave it to him* – see Unit 10).	*believe, see, feel, love*
Intransitive	• Verbs that do not need a direct object in order to make sense. • Some verbs can be transitive or intransitive (e.g. *dance: I dance salsa* vs. *I dance on Saturdays*), and a good dictionary will tell you this.	*talk, laugh, dance, go*
Reflexive	• Verbs that can mean a person is doing the action to themselves. • This is normally expressed through a **reflexive pronoun** (e.g. *himself, herself, themselves*).	*hurt, cut, dress*

■ Verb patterns

> ### Exercise 2
> Look at the underlined parts of the sentences below and answer the questions.
>
> 1 It <u>depends on the weather</u>.
> 2 I <u>believe in</u> good <u>luck</u>.
> 3 I <u>remembered to ask</u> Jane.
> 4 I <u>remember asking</u> Jane.
>
> Is there a preposition after the verb?
> Is there an object after the verb?
> Is there a second verb and what form is it?
>
> Check your answers on page 124.

We use the term **verb pattern** to describe the form of words that often follow particular verbs. For example, *depend* is often followed by the **dependent preposition** *on* but it is not followed by *about*. (A dependent preposition is a preposition that is always used with a particular noun, verb or adjective before another word.)

Some verbs take one or more **object(s)** while others do not need an object. Some verbs need a **complement**, i.e. a phrase that is necessary to complete the meaning of a particular verb in a **clause** or sentence. For example, in the sentence *I am tired,* the adjective *tired* is the complement. Verbs such as *be, feel, become* and *get* need a complement in order to make sense. For example, *she became* has no meaning but *she became **an actor*** does. In this example *an actor* is the complement.

Some verbs are followed by an **infinitive form** (e.g. *I want to go* home), while others are followed by an ***-ing* form** (e.g. *I like living* here). Some verbs can have a different meaning depending on whether they are followed by the infinitive form or the *-ing* form (e.g. *remember*). Verb patterns after **verbs of perception** (verbs related to the senses or emotions such as *hear, see* and *hate*) can affect meaning, for example *I heard him speaking* (I heard the act of speaking in progress) and *I heard him speak* (I heard the complete act of speaking). A good dictionary will tell you the pattern(s) that can follow a verb. (For more information on grammar patterns with verbs and adjectives, see pages 26–7, Unit 5.)

■ Modality

Modality refers to the lexical and grammatical ways a person expresses their attitude to what they say. For example, in *I'm probably going home soon*, the word *probably* is a lexical way of showing that the speaker is uncertain. In *I might go home soon*, the modal verb *might* is a grammatical way of showing the same uncertainty.

Exercise 3

Look at sentences a)–d), which use the modal verbs *can* and *might*. Answer the questions.

a) I finish work at 5.00 so I can go home soon.
b) That letter might have got lost in the post.
c) She might know Peter. I'm not sure.
d) Can you help me, please? I can't find the shampoo.

1 Where is the modal placed in the verb phrase?
2 What form is the verb after the modal?
3 How are questions and negatives formed with a modal?
4 What is the past form?
5 What happens when *she* is used?

Check your answers on page 124.

The nine pure modal verbs (*can, could, may, might, will, would, should, must* and *shall*) do not always behave grammatically in the same way as other verbs. For example, they do not use other auxiliaries to form questions or negatives (see d) in Exercise 3) and they use *have* and a **past participle** when making a past form (see b) in Exercise 3).

There are also **semi-modal** verbs such as *have to, ought to, need to* and *be able to*. These verbs sometimes change their form to show person (*he has to*), have a past form (*he had to*) or use another auxiliary (*he was able to*). Some semi-modal verbs can also behave as pure modal verbs. For example, a question with *need to* can be *Need you go?*

The same modal verb can have different meanings and be used for different **functions**. For example, *can* can mean 'be able' and 'be allowed to' and is used to express ability, ask for permission, give permission, make requests, express possibility and to offer to help. To help you decide what meaning and function a modal has in a sentence, look at the **context**.

Exercise 4

Match the examples of modals on the left with the functions on the right.

Example of modal	*Function*
1 You <u>must</u> always show your passport at the check-in desk.	a) making logical deduction
2 The letter <u>must</u> be lost; they posted it last week.	b) expressing obligation
3 You <u>should</u> see a doctor about those headaches.	c) making requests
4 <u>Could</u> you carry this bag for me, please?	d) asking permission
5 A: <u>May</u> I open the window? B: Sure, go ahead.	e) giving advice

Check your answers on page 124 and read the notes.

For more detailed information on the meaning/use of other modal verbs look in a good grammar reference or in a good dictionary.

■ Forms that express hypothetical meaning

We use the term **hypothetical** for situations that are unreal, imaginary, impossible or unlikely to happen. For example, in *I wish I had lots of money*, the underlined part of the sentence is unreal, it is the opposite of the facts, i.e. the speaker does not have lots of money.

Exercise 5

What types of verb are underlined in sentences 1 and 2 below? What form are the verbs in 3, 4 and 5? For example, *had* in *I wish I had lots of money* is a past simple form.

1 I <u>would</u> never lie to my parents; it's totally unthinkable!
2 Nowadays, I <u>could</u> never stay up all night like I used to when I was younger.
3 Suppose you <u>won</u> $1,000,000 ... I know you won't, but just suppose.
4 If only I <u>hadn't lost</u> my wallet! But there's nothing I can do about it now.
5 I wish I <u>wasn't going</u> to work tomorrow, but I have to.

Now read the next section.

Some modal verbs can be used to express hypothetical meaning; for example, *would* (general hypothetical) and *could* (hypothetical ability). In number 2, if the speaker used *can*, it could mean that staying up all night was something they try but fail to achieve. By changing the form into the past (*could*), the speaker implies that this is something they will not even attempt because it is impossible.

   This change to the past to show that the action or event is hypothetical is true of other verbs. For example, in number 3 the past simple shows that the speaker thinks this is a very unlikely event. If the speaker thought it was more likely, they would use *win*. In number 4, the past perfect (*hadn't lost*) shows that the event in the sentence is unreal because the speaker is imagining a situation when the loss of his wallet had not occurred. To describe a real event he would use the past simple (*I lost my wallet*). Similarly, in number 5 the form changes from present continuous to past continuous. (For more information on **conditional** sentences, see pages 78–9, Unit 14.)

■ Adverbials

Adverbs modify verbs, **adjectives** and other adverbs. In number 1 in Exercise 5, *never* is an adverb of frequency, i.e. it tells us how often the event (lying) happens. There are many kinds of adverb but some are:

- place, e.g. *go there, come here, they live nearby*
- degree, e.g. *he's extremely happy, I'm very excited, she's really ill*
- manner, e.g. *she drives carefully, he walks slowly, we work well together*
- quantity, e.g. *I like tennis a lot, they didn't like London much, we talked a little*
- time, e.g. *Where did you live before?, we bought it recently, I haven't phoned her yet*.

Adverbs can be formed in different ways. One common way is to add *ly* to an adjective (e.g. *quickly*), but some adverbs are not formed from adjectives (e.g. *very*). Other adverbs have the same form as the adjective; for example, *I tried hard* (adverb) *in the hard* (adjective) *exam*. Adverbs are placed in different parts of a sentence and a good grammar will tell you the possibilities.

Adverbial clauses are groups of one or more words that act as adverbs. For example, in *I arrived at the party before you did*, the underlined part is an adverbial clause: it tells us when I arrived at the party. Adverbs and adverbial clauses are both categorised as **adverbials**, i.e. words or groups of words that act adverbially.

■ Passive voice

The voice of a verb form gives information about who did and who 'received' an action. In the **active voice**, the **subject** of the sentence is the person who did the action and the object is the person who received the action: *He [subject] told me [object] to leave the building*. In the **passive voice** the subject is the person who received the action: *I [subject] was told to leave the building (by him)*. In both sentences, the person doing the action is the same (*he/him*) but the structure of the sentence has changed.

The passive voice is commonly formed by using the auxiliary *be* (e.g. *was*) or *be* with another auxiliary (e.g. *have been, can't be*) and the past participle (e.g. *told*). We do not normally use perfect continuous forms in the passive voice because the structure becomes long and *be* has to be repeated as an auxiliary (e.g. *I have been being driven* (✗)).

Exercise 6

Look at the sentences below and decide why the passive voice has been used in each.

1 Tickets <u>must be bought</u> from official ticket agencies only.
2 First, the coffee beans <u>are picked</u> and then <u>roasted</u> in ovens.
3 I know very little about coffee but I'm sure it <u>can't be grown</u> in Europe!
4 I'm sorry but my essay <u>won't be finished</u> today.
5 I <u>was</u> very <u>amused</u> by the film that we watched at your house the other night.

Now read the next section.

The passive voice can be used for a number of different reasons. For example, when the person who does the action is obvious (in number 1 in Exercise 6 it is obvious that 'we' buy the tickets), when the person doing the action is not important (numbers 1 and 2) or when we are describing a process (number 2). The passive is also used when we want to begin a phrase or sentence with a topic we already know. For example, in number 3, *it* refers to *coffee* which we already know about; using the active voice would mean beginning the phrase with *people*, which is a change in topic. We can also use the passive when we want to avoid showing responsibility for something and distance ourselves from an action. (In number 4, the speaker knows that the action is bad and so wants to remove their responsibility.) The passive can also be used to avoid having long noun phrases as the subject. (In number 5, using the active voice would mean writing *The film that I saw at your house the other night amused me.*) In addition, the passive voice can be used when the style is formal (number 1) and it is typical of formal notices, newspaper reports and academic writing.

We can use the verb *get* as an auxiliary instead of *be* in the passive voice (e.g. *I got cut off when I was on the phone*). We often use *get* when the event is accidental, we can't control it, or it is irritating.

We can also use *have/get* in the passive voice to show that something or someone else did the action or caused the action to happen (e.g. *I got my hair cut / I had my hair cut*). This is sometimes called the **causative passive**.

For fuller and more detailed information on the passive and all other areas covered in this unit, you should look at a good grammar reference.

> **FOLLOW-UP ACTIVITIES** *(See page 124 for answers)*

1 In the dialogue below, find examples of:

the auxiliaries *be*, *do* and *have*	*be*, *do* and *have* as main verbs
adverbs of frequency and place	the passive voice
a modal verb	

A: Are you going out tonight?
B: Yes, with John. Do you mind?
A: No, of course not. I was just asking. I'm always interested in what you do!
B: John's been given some free tickets to a club in the city centre. We've arranged to meet some friends there.
A: It sounds great. I hope you have a good time. Can you call me tomorrow?
B: Yes, sure.

2 What functions do the modal and semi-modal verbs in the sentences below express?
   1 You have to turn the volume up if you want to hear the TV.
   2 You have to show the man your ticket before you get on the train.
   3 You mustn't worry; everything's fine.
   4 You must know Jane: you went to school with her.

DISCOVERY ACTIVITIES

1 Choose an area of grammar discussed in this unit that you found difficult and use the two references below to find out more about it. Which reference did you find more useful?
Cambridge Grammar of English by Ronald Carter and Michael McCarthy, Cambridge University Press 2006
Grammar for English Language Teachers (Second Edition) by Martin Parrott, Cambridge University Press 2010

2 Choose two areas of grammar discussed in this unit that you found interesting. Look at a written text (e.g. a newspaper) and underline examples of the grammar areas. For example, if you chose passives, find passive structures in the text.

TKT: KAL practice task 12 *(See page 133 for answers)*

A teacher is researching different forms of verbs.

For items **1-5**, read the questions about forms of verbs and choose which of the options (**A**, **B** or **C**) is **NOT** an example of the form.

1 Which of the following is <u>NOT</u> an example of an auxiliary verb?

  A   He was very boring.

  B   He was living in London.

  C   He was told to be quiet.

2 Which of the following is <u>NOT</u> an example of the passive voice?

  A   It was sold to my father.

  B   It was taken to the garage and fixed.

  C   It was spoken English she found most difficult.

3 Which of the following is <u>NOT</u> an example of a past modal?

  A   You can't have eaten my chocolate!

  B   You mustn't eat my chocolate!

  C   You ate my chocolate! You really shouldn't have!

4 Which of the following is <u>NOT</u> an example of a verb + dependent preposition?

  A   I believe in you, I really do.

  B   You really should listen to me more.

  C   Let's meet at five. Don't be late!

5 Which of the following is <u>NOT</u> an example of an action verb?

  A   I could dress myself when I was five.

  B   I don't really belong here.

  C   Sorry, I broke the lamp.

Unit 13   The form, meaning and use of structural patterns using verbs

LEARNING OUTCOME

KNOWLEDGE: the form, meaning and use of verbs and grammatical structures in the present, past and future

■ Grammatical form/structure, meaning and use

We use the terms 'grammatical form' and **grammatical structure** to refer to a grammatical language pattern and the parts which combine to make it. For example, in *I am getting on the train*, the grammatical structure is the **present continuous** and the **form** is **subject** + (**auxiliary verb**) *be* + *-ing* **form** (**present participle**).

The term 'use' refers to the meaning that is expressed by the grammatical structure. Many people use 'meaning' and 'use' to mean the same thing. The meaning/use of the present continuous can be to describe an action happening now, for example (while on a mobile phone) *I'm getting on the train so I can't talk to you*. The meaning/use of a grammatical structure often depends on the **context** in which it is used because one structure can have more than one meaning/use.

■ Time and tense

> **Exercise 1**
> What do the underlined parts of the verbs below tell you about time?
>
> 1 he live<u>s</u>   2 he liv<u>ed</u>   3 he <u>will</u> live
>
> Now read the next section.

Tense refers to how the form of a **verb** expresses time. In English, there are only two tenses, present and past, because the verb form itself does not change to express the future; auxiliaries are used instead, for example *he live<u>s</u>* (present), *he liv<u>ed</u>* (past), but *he <u>will</u> live* (future). However, many coursebooks refer to a large selection of grammatical structures as tenses, for example the present continuous, the **present simple** and the **future with** *going to*.

There is often no obvious connection between the tense of a verb and the time it expresses. For example, in *The class begins at nine*, the tense is present simple but the time it expresses is the future.

■ Aspect: perfect and continuous

Exercise 2

Look at the dialogue below about living in London. Which of the underlined parts tells us that the action is temporary and which links the past to the present?

A: Do you like it here?
B: I love it. <u>I've lived</u> here for ages. What about you?
A: Yes, I really like it. <u>I'm living</u> with some friends because I'm only here for a few months; my permanent home is in New York.

Now read the next section.

The term **aspect** refers to how we express if an event is long or short, completed or continuing, repeated, temporary, etc., independently of the time of the event. English has two aspects: continuous (or progressive) and perfect. The continuous aspect is formed from the auxiliary *be* and a present participle (*I'm living*) and the perfect aspect from the auxiliary *have* and a **past participle** (*I've lived*).

The continuous aspect in *I'm living with some friends* expresses the idea that this event is temporary. The continuous aspect can also be used to express the idea that an action is ongoing or repeated. The perfect aspect in *I've lived here for ages* expresses the idea that the event continues from the past to the present. We can also use the continuous aspect with the perfect aspect. In this case, the auxiliary *be* from the continuous is used in its past participle form, for example *I've been driving all night*. When we combine the two aspects we can express **complex** meanings. For example, *I'll have been working here for nine years in May* (future perfect continuous) connects two points in the future while also showing that the action is ongoing.

Exercise 3

Look at the sentences containing the perfect aspect below and decide what the underlined forms express. For example, *I've lived* relates the past to the present. That is, the event began in the past and continues now.

1 <u>I've lived</u> in Rome for years.
2 <u>I'll have been</u> in this house five years by the end of March.
3 <u>Kate's travelled</u> a lot with her parents.
4 <u>She'd been</u> to Paris twice before she was 15.

Check your answers on pages 124–5 and read the notes. For further information on the form and use of the continuous aspect, read the following sections.

■ The meanings/uses of present forms

Exercise 4

Look at the sentences below and decide what meanings the underlined forms express. Use the context to help you decide.

1 My sister is staying with me at the moment.
2 I take the bus every day to my office.
3 I'm going to India next year for my holiday; I booked it yesterday.
4 The train leaves at seven o'clock; we'd better hurry.
5 The Nile is the longest river in the world.
6 The sun is shining and the birds are singing. Wish you were here. Love John xx

Now read the next section.

The underlined structures in Exercise 4 are present forms but they do not have a present meaning or use in all the sentences. For example, in number 4 the present simple (*The train leaves*) is used to express the idea of timetabled time, i.e. something fixed that will happen in the future. Some different meanings/uses of present forms are summarised in the table below. (For information on the present perfect form and meaning/use, see the key to Exercise 3 on pages 124–5.)

Term	Examples	Uses
Present simple	*I take the bus every day to my office.*	To describe a routine action or a habit.
	The train leaves at seven o'clock.	To describe an event which is fixed by a timetable and unchanging (until the timetable changes). In this example it is also used to describe something happening in the future.
	The Nile is the longest river in the world.	To describe a fact, something that is always true.
Present continuous/ progressive	*My sister is staying with me at the moment.*	To describe an action happening now, which is temporary.
	The sun is shining and the birds are singing.	To describe a background situation, 'paint a picture' for the listener/reader. (The action is happening now from the speaker's/writer's point of view.)
	I'm having a bad time with my neighbours at the moment.	To describe an action happening around the present time which is ongoing and temporary (though not necessarily happening at the exact moment of speaking).
	I'm going to India next year.	To describe a future action that is planned or is a strong intention.

■ The meanings/uses of past forms

Exercise 5

Look at the sentences below and decide what meanings the underlined forms express. Use the context to help you decide. Then use the underlined forms to complete the table below. We have done the first one for you.

1 I lived in Singapore last year but I'm back in London now.
2 I was walking down the road when I met John and stopped to talk.
3 If I won a million dollars tomorrow, I'd buy a big house. No chance of that though!
4 The band was playing and lots of people were dancing. It was such a great party!
5 At this time yesterday, I was having dinner in Paris! I wish I was still there now.
6 Every summer, we went to my grandparents' house. We used to drive there.

Check your answers on page 125.

Term	Examples	Uses
Past simple	I lived in Singapore last year.	To describe an action/event that started and finished in the past. Often with a time reference e.g. *last year*.
	1 _____ _____	To describe a future action which is unreal, imaginary, or part of a conditional structure (see Unit 14).
	2 _____ _____	To describe a present action or state which is unreal or imaginary.
	3 _____ _____	To describe a past routine or habit, repeated in the past (but not now).
Used to + infinitive	4 _____ _____	To describe a past routine, habit or state, repeated in the past (but not now).
Past continuous/ progressive	5 _____ _____	To describe a background action or situation that is interrupted by a second action.
	6 _____ _____	To describe a background situation in the past, to 'paint a picture' for the listener/ reader.
	7 _____	To describe a longer action that happened around a point of time in the past, i.e. it began before and continued after this time. (In this case the event is also temporary.)

Previously, we saw how present forms do not always express present time. The same is true of past forms. (Note: information on the **past perfect simple** form and meaning/ use is included in the key to Exercise 3 on page 125.)

■ How present and past forms are made

Exercise 6

Look at the sentences below and label the underlined parts, for example *subject, auxiliary, main verb*.

1 He went to Singapore on holiday last year but normally he goes to Italy.
2 I'm having dinner at home tonight but this time yesterday I was having dinner in Paris!

Now check your answers in the table below and read the notes on page 125.

Declarative (statement forms) (see page 77, Unit 14)

Name of form	Subject	Auxiliary	Main verb (present simple / past simple / present participle)
Present/Past simple	He		went (past simple) to Singapore ... goes (present simple) to Italy.
Present/Past continuous	I	'm/was	having (present participle) dinner in Paris!

Exercise 7

Look at the underlined parts of the sentences below and use them to complete the information in the two tables below. If necessary, look at the table above and the tables in the key for Exercise 3 on page 125 for some help with labelling the different parts.

1 I don't/didn't want to leave Singapore.
2 I'm not / I wasn't working because of the power cut.
3 When do/did they go to Singapore?
4 Where were you living when you were in New York?

Negative

Name of form	_____	_____ + not	Main verb: base form OR _____
Present/Past simple	I	_____	want (base form)
Present/Past continuous	I	am ('m) not / wasn't	_____

Interrogative (question forms) (see page 77, Unit 14)

Name of form	Question word	_____	_____	_____ OR present participle
Present/Past simple	When	_____	they	_____?
Present/Past continuous	Where	_____	you	_____?

Check your answers on pages 125–6 and read the notes.

When forming a question (interrogative) or a negative with present or past forms, we often use the auxiliaries *do* or *be*. We don't use them when we use *be* as a main verb, for example *Which is the longest river in the world?*

When a **wh- word** is the subject of a present or past simple question we do not use an auxiliary. We use the third person singular form of the verb. For example: *What comes/came first, the meat or the soup?* not *What does/did come first?* (✗)

■ The meanings/uses of future forms

Previously, we saw that present and past forms can be used to talk about the future. There are also other **future forms** in English which express different meanings/uses.

Exercise 8

Look at the three future structures below and decide what meaning/use the underlined forms express. Use the context to help you decide.

Future with *will/shall*: *will/shall* + base form
1 <u>I'll be</u> forty-three on my next birthday.
2 <u>Will Manchester United win</u> the match on Saturday, do you think?

Future continuous: *will/shall* + *be* + present participle
3 This time tomorrow, <u>I'll be driving</u> home, I think.
4 <u>I'll be seeing</u> the doctor again next Friday; I've got an appointment.

***Be going to* + base form**
5 It's very dark! <u>It's going to rain</u>.
6 I've decided <u>we're going to buy</u> a new car next year.

Check your answers in the tables on page 126. (Note: information on the future perfect form and meaning/use is included in the key to Exercise 3 on pages 124–5.)

There are a number of other forms used to express the present, past and future. There are also other ways in which the forms above can be used. For more information on these forms, you should look at a good grammar reference.

FOLLOW-UP ACTIVITIES *(See page 126 for answers)*

1 Identify the grammatical structures below, e.g. subject + auxiliary *was/were* + present participle = *past continuous declarative*.
   1 auxiliary *did* + subject + base form = _____
   2 subject + *will* + *be* + present participle = _____
   3 *will* + subject + base form = _____
   4 subject + auxiliary *do/does* + *not* + base form = _____

2 Match forms 1–4 with the meanings/uses a)–d).
   1 Present continuous   a) Relates a point in the past to another point in the past
   2 Present perfect   b) Relates the past to the present
   3 *Used to* + base form   c) A past routine, habit or state, repeated in the past (but not continued in the present)
   4 Past perfect   d) A future action that is planned or is a strong intention

> **DISCOVERY ACTIVITIES**
>
> 1 Look at a written text (e.g. a newspaper) and underline all the present, past and/ or future forms. Use the context to decide what meaning the writer is expressing by using these forms.
> 2 Choose a grammatical structure that you find difficult and write a factsheet including information about its use and form. Then compare your factsheet with a grammar reference. Is the information the same? What, if anything, did you miss out?

TKT: KAL practice task 13 *(See page 133 for answers)*

A teacher is reading her students' homework and has written comments to help them correct their work.

For questions **1-7**, match the teacher's comments with the examples from students' work listed **A-H**.

There is one extra option which you do not need to use.

Examples from students' work

> **A** Are you agree with me?
> **B** Do you are happy or not?
> **C** Who did want to speak to me yesterday?
> **D** We're going to having a party next Sunday.
> **E** I'll be living in London by this time next year.
> **F** We didn't used to like vegetables when we were children, did we?
> **G** I will go to a football match on Saturday; I bought the tickets yesterday.
> **H** I've been to Moscow last year and it was great.

Teacher's comments

1 We don't normally use the future with *will* here. The present continuous is better.
2 In past simple subject questions, you don't need the auxiliary.
3 You need to use the base form after this form.
4 We use the auxiliary *do* in present simple questions.
5 When *be* is a main verb, you don't need to use an auxiliary.
6 Be careful. You need to change the form of this verb in past simple negatives.
7 We normally use the past simple, not the present perfect simple, with a specific past time.

Unit 14   Sentences and clauses

LEARNING OUTCOME

KNOWLEDGE: how different sentences and clauses are formed, what they mean and how they can combine

■ What are sentences and clauses?

In Units 11 and 12 we looked at **noun phrases** and **verb phrases**. For example, in *I had to leave the room* there is a verb phrase (*had to leave*) and two noun phrases (*I, the room*). Phrases generally cannot stand alone but are part of longer units of language. These longer units are often called sentences and clauses.

A sentence is the largest unit of grammar and normally has, at least, a **subject** and **finite verb** (a verb form that shows its time or **person**). For example, *I had to leave the room* is a sentence because it has a subject (*I*) and a finite verb (*had*).

A **clause** normally has a verb and often has a subject; for example, *I had to leave the room* is a clause as well as a sentence. However, the verb in a clause does not have to be finite. For example, in *I had to leave the room to fetch my book* the underlined part is a clause but not a sentence because it has a **non-finite verb** (*to fetch*), which does not show its tense. It also has no subject.

A sentence has at least one clause. *I had to leave the room* is a one-clause sentence and *I had to leave the room to fetch my book* is a two-clause sentence in which a finite clause is followed by a non-finite clause.

Exercise 1
How many clauses are there in the following sentence? Are they finite or non-finite?

John was reading quietly when I walked into the room, so I went outside again to make a phone call.

Check your answers on page 126.

■ Types of sentences and clauses

In Exercise 1, *John was reading quietly* and *I went outside again* are called **main clauses**. You can also have **subordinate clauses**. The differences are listed in the table below.

Main clause	Subordinate clause
John was reading quietly / I went outside again	*when I walked into the room / to make a phone call*
• It can stand alone. • It is not dependent on other clauses for its meaning. • It has at least a subject and a verb.	• It cannot stand alone. • It is dependent on other clauses for its meaning. • It adds meaning to other clauses.

You can also describe sentences as follows:

Simple sentence	Compound sentence	Complex sentence
John was reading quietly.	John was reading quietly, so I went outside again.	John was reading quietly when I walked into the room.
• It has only one main clause with subject + verb + object or adverb.	• It has two main clauses.	• It has at least one main clause and at least one subordinate clause, which can sometimes appear in any order, e.g. *John was reading quietly when I walked into the room. / When I walked into the room, John was reading quietly.*

Exercise 2

Underline the main and subordinate clauses in the sentences below. Are the sentences simple, compound or complex?

1 As I get older, I can't work so hard.
2 John left the house and I left about ten minutes later.
3 The man who spoke to me was very helpful.
4 To help my students, I correct all homework carefully.

Check your answers on pages 126–7 and read the notes with them.

Clauses are often joined together by **conjunctions** (**connectors**) that show how one clause connects to the other. For example, in number 1 above, the clauses are joined by the conjunction *as*. This is a **subordinating conjunction** joining a subordinate clause (*I get older*) to a main clause (*I can't work so hard*). Notice that the conjunction still 'joins' the clauses even though, physically, it is not between them; the sentence could be rewritten *I can't work so hard as I get older*. The relationship expressed by *as* is 'time', i.e. <u>during the time that</u> *I get older*. In number 2, *and* is a **co-ordinating conjunction**. Co-ordinating conjunctions are used to join main clauses and, again, show the relationship between them. In this example *and* expresses addition.

Exercise 3

In the sentences below, what is the connection expressed by the underlined parts?

1 John was reading quietly <u>when</u> I walked into the room.
2 John was reading quietly, <u>so</u> I went outside again.
3 I went outside again <u>because</u> John was reading quietly.
4 I went outside again <u>to make</u> a phone call.

Check your answers on page 127.

Other examples of subordinating conjunctions are *although, if, before* and *whereas*. Other examples of co-ordinating conjunctions are *but* and *or*. An **infinitive of purpose** can also be used to join clauses together as in number 4 above (*to make*). (For more information on conjunctions, see page 88, Unit 16.)

As well as subordinate, main, simple or complex, there are four other ways of describing the form of a clause or sentence:

Declarative	Interrogative	Imperative	Exclamative
I left the room.	Why did you make a phone call?	Leave the room, please.	What a noisy phone call!
In the form of statements	In the form of questions	In the form of orders	In the form of exclamations

Negative forms are used in the first three types; for example, *I didn't leave the room* is a negative **declarative** sentence. Negative forms are not normally used in exclamatives. The **form** may not always relate to the meaning/use. For example, the **interrogative** sentence above could be complaining or expressing irritation; the meaning could be: *You're always making phone calls. Who are you speaking to?*

■ Relative clauses

In Unit 11, we saw that one way of modifying nouns or noun phrases is to use **relative clauses** and there is an example of a relative clause in Exercise 2: *who spoke to me*.

Exercise 4

Which underlined relative clause in the sentences below tells us which person or thing we are referring to and which adds extra information?

1   A lot of the staff in that shop are rather rude but the woman <u>who served me</u> was very friendly.
2   My neighbour, <u>who has lived next door for many years</u>, has sold his house.

Now read the next section.

Number 1 above is a defining relative clause; it defines the noun phrase (*the woman*). In number 2, the underlined part is a non-defining relative clause. It does not tell us which neighbour we are referring to: it adds extra information about him. Non-defining relative clauses are separated from the main clause by commas but defining relative clauses are not. Relative clauses can appear in the middle of a main clause or come after it but they cannot come before it. Relative clauses often start with a **relative pronoun** such as *who*, *that* and *which*.

Exercise 5

Can the relative pronoun be omitted from the defining relative clauses below?

1   The woman <u>who I served</u> was very friendly.
2   The woman <u>who served me</u> was very friendly.

Now read the next section.

Relative pronouns can sometimes be omitted in defining relative clauses. For example, in number 1 above, *who* can be omitted because it refers to the **object** of the relative clause, i.e. *I served <u>the woman</u>* (object). However, in number 2, *who* cannot be omitted because it is the subject of the relative clause (<u>the woman</u> *served me*). Relative pronouns cannot be omitted in non-defining relative clauses.

It is not always necessary to use a complete relative clause in a sentence. For example, in *The woman working in that shop is very nice*, the relative clause is not complete, i.e. the full form is *The woman who is working in that shop is very nice*. This is called a **reduced relative clause** and is made by removing the **pronoun** and **auxiliary verb**, which we do not need in order to understand the sentence.

■ Conditionals

In Unit 12, we saw that the term **hypothetical** is used to describe situations that are untrue, imagined, impossible or unlikely to happen. We use the term **conditional** to refer to **grammatical structures** that describe events or situations that can happen only if something else happens. For example, in *If I won the lottery, I'd buy a big house* the second event will happen only if the first event happens. In this case, both events are very unlikely to happen so the sentence is conditional *and* hypothetical.

Exercise 6

Look at the sentences below and decide if the events are real/unreal, likely/unlikely or possible/impossible by circling one word in the brackets after each clause. What time (past, present, future, all time) do the sentences refer to?

1 If the sun shines (*real/unreal*), people are happy (*real/unreal*).
2 If it rains tomorrow (*possible/impossible*), I'll stay at home (*likely/unlikely*).
3 If I was younger (*possible/impossible*), I would be more adventurous (*likely/unlikely*).
4 If I got the job (*likely/unlikely*), I'd earn a lot more money (*likely/unlikely*).
5 If she had seen you (*possible/impossible*), she would have said hello (*possible/impossible*).

Check your answers and read the notes on page 127.

Some people call the part of the sentence with *if* the 'if clause' while others call it the 'conditional clause'. Some people call the part of the sentence without *if* the conditional clause. Whatever their labels, the part of the sentence with *if* is a subordinate clause and the other part is a main clause. To avoid confusion, we will refer to the '*if* clause' and the 'main clause'.

The conditional sentences in Exercise 6 are often called: zero conditional; **Type 1 or first conditional**; **Type 2 or second conditional**; **Type 3 or third conditional**. The table below shows the basic forms of these conditionals.

Sentence in Exercise 6	Type of conditional	If clause form	Main clause form
1	Zero (real)	Present	Present
2	Type 1 / first conditional (possible/likely/real)	Present	Future
3 and 4	Type 2 / second conditional (unlikely/unreal)	Past	*Would* + base form
5	Type 3 / third conditional (impossible)	Past perfect	*Would* + *have* + past participle

There are a number of verb forms you can use in each type of conditional. For example, you do not have to use the **present simple** and *will* in a Type 1. Instead you can use the **present continuous/progressive**, *be going to*, the **present perfect** or another **modal verb** that expresses the future (e.g. *if you're having dinner, I can call later*), or an **imperative**. For this reason, the table on page 78 simply states 'present' rather than naming a form. In Type 2 conditionals, you can use other past forms instead of the **past simple**. You can use the **past continuous/progressive** and *was going to* (but not the **past perfect**), for example. You can use *were* with *I* in this type of conditional (e.g. *If I were younger*) and *would* can be replaced by *could* or *might*. In Type 3 conditionals, you cannot use a form other than the past perfect in the *if* clause but *would* can be replaced by *could* or *might*.

As well as *if*, you can use other conjunctions in the *if* clause (e.g. *when, as long as, if only, unless, supposing*) depending on the meaning you want to express. You cannot, however, use all these conjunctions in all types of conditional.

The two clauses can be in any order but we use a comma between them when the *if* clause comes first. Sometimes, the *if* clause can be omitted when it is already understood, for example A: *I wasn't well last week.* B: *Why didn't you tell me? I'd have come round* (i.e. if you had told me you weren't well).

As well as variations in the form, some of the conditional types can be mixed together to express different meanings. These are called **mixed conditionals**. For example:

If clause (Type 3)	Main clause (Type 2)
1 If you hadn't saved all that cash,	we wouldn't be in our new house now.
If clause (Type 2)	Main clause (Type 3)
2 If you weren't so tired all the time,	I'd have bought you dinner last night.

(based on *Grammar for English Language Teachers (Second Edition)* by Martin Parrott, Cambridge University Press 2010)

1 a past action (*you saved cash*) + a present result (*we are in our new house*)
2 a present or general fact (*you are tired*) + a past result (*I didn't buy you dinner*)

As well as expressing different times and levels of reality, likelihood and possibility, conditionals are used to express various **functions**.

Exercise 7

What functions do the conditional sentences below express? For example, *If I had a bigger house, I'd be so happy! = wishing, dreaming*.

1   If you don't call soon, I'll never speak to you again.
2   If I hadn't lost that watch she gave me, I wouldn't feel so guilty now.
3   Sorry, but if my train hadn't broken down, I'd have been here earlier.
4   If I were you, I'd go and see a doctor.

Check your answers on page 127.

■ Reported speech and reporting verbs

We use the term **direct speech** to refer to the actual words people say, for example *'I want to go home'*. **Reported speech** or indirect speech is how we report what someone says, for example *She said that she wanted to go home*. It is often used in newspaper/radio/TV reports, in stories and when talking about conversations we heard or something we read.

Exercise 8

Look at the direct and reported speech sentences below and make notes about the changes made.

Direct speech	Reported speech	Changes
1 'I want to go home.'	She said that she wanted to go home.	
2 'We've been to Paris.'	He told me that they had been to Paris.	
3 'I was talking to you.'	He claimed that he had been talking to me.	
4 'Can you come?'	He asked me if I could come.	
5 'You must finish early.'	He warned us that we had to finish early.	

Check your answers by reading the table and notes about changes on pages 127–8.

When using reported speech, we often make changes to the grammatical structures in the sentence. For example, the present simple becomes the past simple. We can also change other parts of the sentence such as the time reference. For example, *I want to go home <u>tomorrow</u>* becomes *He said that he wanted to go home <u>the next day</u>*. (For more information on changes made in reported speech, see the Points to note on pages 127–8.)

Reporting verbs are verbs that we commonly use when reporting what someone has said. The reporting verbs in Exercise 8 are *said, told, claimed, asked* and *warned* but there are a number of others. Some reporting verbs express the function of what the original speaker said or how the person reporting interpreted the speaker's words (e.g. *warned* and *claimed*) but some are neutral (e.g. *said, told*). Reporting verbs are followed by different syntactical patterns. For example, *ask* can be followed by **indirect object + infinitive form** (e.g. *he asked me to try harder*) and *said* can be followed by (*that*) + subject + verb phrase (e.g. *she said that she wanted to go home*).

For fuller and more detailed information on the topics covered in this unit, you should look at a good grammar reference.

FOLLOW-UP ACTIVITIES *(See page 128 for answers)*

1 Underline the subordinate clauses in the sentences below and explain their relationship to the main clause.
   1 My sister told me the good news as soon as I got home.
   2 When will you be coming home to see us?
   3 The house where I used to live is just round the corner.
   4 Although I don't really want to, I'm going to have to work late tonight.

2 What type of conditional (0, 1, 2, or 3) is each sentence below?
  1 When the soup is boiling, it's ready to serve.
  2 What could you do if you were asked to leave the company?
  3 She told me to take a break if I wanted to.
  4 If you'd told me sooner, I might have been able to help you.

DISCOVERY ACTIVITIES

1 Choose an area of grammar discussed in this unit that you found difficult and use the two references below to find out more about it. Which reference did you find more useful?
  Uncovering Grammar by Scott Thornbury, Macmillan 2001
  Grammar for English Language Teachers (Second Edition) by Martin Parrott, Cambridge University Press 2010

2 Look at two or three coursebooks that are used in your school and find references to the areas covered in this unit. These might be in individual units of the coursebook or in the grammar references at the end of the coursebooks. Is there anything you would add to the information they give students? Why?

TKT: KAL practice task 14 *(See page 133 for answers)*

A teacher is writing some comments for her students about their homework.

For questions **1-6**, match the teacher's comments with the sentences from students' work listed **A-G**.

There is one extra option which you do not need to use.

Sentences from students' work

A I had to do it myself as my friend wouldn't help me.
B If you will win loads of money, you will be rich.
C I'll never forget the man who saved my life.
D The shop that I normally go to was closed.
E You'll tell me if you have time, won't you?
F My sister, who is older than me, has two children.
G I wrote to Jane to tell her that I was visiting next week.

Teacher's comments

1 It's not wrong but you don't have to use a relative pronoun here.
2 This is a really good use of a conjunction to show reason.
3 We don't use the future with *will* in the first clause here.
4 An excellent use of a non-defining relative clause. Well done.
5 Good that you've used the infinitive to show purpose.
6 A really good example of a conditional sentence.

What is discourse?

Discourse is a connected piece of spoken or written language which is produced in order to communicate. A letter, a short note, a lecture and a conversation are all examples of discourse. **Lexis**, grammar and **phonology** all work together to produce discourse.

Unit 15 Features of common written and spoken text types

LEARNING OUTCOME

KNOWLEDGE: how features combine to create text types and key terms associated with these features

■ What is a text type?

The term **text type** is used to describe a type of text (which can be spoken or written) that is familiar to a particular group of people. For example, recipes are a text type, and so are scientific reports, business presentations and pop songs.

■ Features of common text types

Text types follow patterns of lexis, grammar and organisation that can be predicted by the reader or listener. For example, in the UK, an English-language TV news broadcast will normally begin with the headlines and will then go on to provide more detail of each story. The broadcast might end with sports stories, a weather forecast and a repetition of the headlines. This discourse 'structure' is referred to as 'organisation'.

We also might expect to find **grammatical structures** such as the **present perfect simple** and **continuous** to talk about recent activities, the **past simple** to describe the main events and the **present continuous/progressive** to talk about changes happening now. We can predict these things because we are familiar with the text type and with the **context** of the broadcast, for example which language and country the broadcast is in and who the audience is.

Exercise 1

Look at the two extracts below and make notes on the organisation, lexis and grammatical structures of each one. Compare your answers with those on page 128.

Extract 1 Recipe

4 oz (125 g) pastry (in sheets)
olive oil
6 oz (175 g) cheese, finely grated
freshly ground black pepper

Cut the sheets of pastry in half. Brush each one with olive oil, then fold in half and brush with oil again. Place a narrow band of grated cheese along one edge and grind black pepper over the top. Roll up tightly. Cut the roll in half and brush the top with olive oil. Repeat with the remaining sheets. Place on a greased baking sheet and bake at 220 °C/427 °F/gas 7 for 15 minutes. Eat hot, or while still warm from the oven.

(based on *Linda's Kitchen* by Linda McCartney, Little, Brown and Company (Inc.) 1995)

Extract 2 Letter/email of complaint

I am writing to complain about the unacceptable service I received in your Sevenoaks branch on 14th August. While attempting to pay for my purchases, I was informed by one of your staff that I would not be allowed to buy the item I had chosen unless I could provide evidence of my age. Unfortunately, I did not have the identification documents asked for and as a result was refused the item. I was embarrassed to be treated in such a way as I am 36 years old and clearly not under the age at which such purchases are prohibited. I left the store feeling humiliated.

While I understand that laws are not created by your company, I do feel that your employees should be more flexible when the person in question is clearly older than 18. I expect an apology at your earliest convenience.

I look forward to hearing from you soon.

Extract 1:

Extract 2:

In written or spoken text types, you also need to take into account the audience (the person or people a text is produced for) and the relationship the writer/speaker has with the audience. For example, notice the formality of the language used in the letter/email of complaint. The writer uses *informed* rather than *told* and the full **forms** of verbs rather than **contractions**. This is because the writer is writing to someone they do not know about a serious issue (see the section about **register** below). In addition, the purpose of the text will affect the language used. For example, does the writer/speaker want to persuade the audience, advise them or to inform them of something?

In many written text types **layout** (how the text looks on the page) is also important. For example, in a cookery recipe, we expect to see pictures and lists. In an email, we expect to see an address and subject line, while in a letter, we expect to see the sender's address in the top right-hand corner and the date under it.

■ Sentences and utterances

A sentence is the largest unit of grammar and normally has, at least, a **subject** and **finite verb** (see page 75, Unit 14). For example, *I live in London* is a sentence. Sentences can be written or spoken.

In spoken discourse, sentences can be difficult to identify because they are broken by pauses or interrupted by other speakers or because sometimes people do not speak in whole sentences. For example, the second part of the following **dialogue** is not a whole sentence:

A: Do you like coffee?
B: Yes.

Partly for these reasons, a spoken 'sentence' is often called an **utterance**. An utterance can be defined as a complete unit of speech in spoken language, a piece of speech that has a beginning and an end. So, in the dialogue above, both *Do you like coffee?* and *Yes* are utterances but only the first is a sentence.

■ Register

In Exercise 1, the different text types used language in different ways. For example, in the letter of complaint, the grammatical structures were more complex than in the recipe.

Exercise 2
Look at the sentences and utterances below and answer the questions.

1 I would like to enquire about the post of ...
2 Hi. How are you doing?
3 In this essay, I will demonstrate that ...
4 Would passengers for Northampton, please proceed to platform 5 immediately.

a) Are they spoken or written?
b) What text type might they come from?
c) Are they formal or informal? How do you know?

Compare your answers with those on page 129.

Register and **style** affect the kind of language used in a text. For example, they affect how **formal** or **informal** the language is, how **complex** or simple the grammar or lexis is (complicated grammatical structures with a number of parts (e.g. *I was wondering if you could …?* vs. the more simple *Can you …?* or *enquire* vs. *ask*), how complex the sentence structures are (e.g. the number of **main** and **subordinate clauses**) and whether contractions and abbreviations are used. Register is also used to describe the words used by a particular group of people. For example, doctors use *diagnose*, while *find out about* is the term more generally used (see pages 7–8, Unit 1).

FOLLOW-UP ACTIVITIES *(See page 129 for answers)*

1 Look at the text types below and match them with the possible features.

Text type	Possible feature	
A human interest story in a newspaper An email to a friend Notes taken during a lecture An academic essay A shopping list	Pictures Columns Bullet points Complex grammar Simple grammar Abbreviations	Contractions Short paragraphs Long paragraphs Direct speech Reported speech

2 Write the formal or informal equivalent of the sentences and utterances below.

Context	Formal	Informal
Meeting someone for the first time	1 How do you do?	_____
Written invitation to dinner	2 We request the pleasure of your company at a dinner to celebrate …	_____ _____ _____
Ending a letter	3 Yours sincerely, …	_____
Beginning a letter	4 _____	Hi Lucy, …

DISCOVERY ACTIVITIES

1 Before you read or listen to a text for the first time, set yourself a discourse-related task. For example: how is the text organised? What is its layout? How does the audience affect the lexis? What is the register (i.e. is it formal/informal, is the lexis typical of a particular job, topic area, etc.)?

2 Look at the list of text types below. Then find a sample of three of them in English and circle examples of the features you listed.

- A film review
- A job advertisement
- A breakfast cereal advertisement
- A description of a hotel on the hotel's website

....

TKT: KAL practice task 15 *(See page 133 for answers)*

A teacher is writing guidelines for her students on features that can make written and spoken discourse more or less formal.

For questions **1-6**, look at the example sentences and match them with the guidelines listed **A**, **B** or **C**. You will need to use some options more than once.

Guidelines for students

A	Using this modal makes the sentence more formal.
B	Using contractions of an auxiliary can make the sentence less formal.
C	The passive voice can sometimes make a sentence sound more formal.

Example sentences

1 Could you help me, please?

2 I can't stay awake any more, so I'm going to bed.

3 Sorry, this isn't my coat, I'm afraid. Would you give it to that lady there?

4 Has he arrived yet? When is he expected?

5 The match is finished. We've missed it.

6 Have we been given permission to land?

....

Unit 16 Coherence and cohesion

LEARNING OUTCOME

KNOWLEDGE: how features combine to create a coherent and cohesive text and key terms associated with coherence and cohesion

What are coherence and cohesion?

Coherence and **cohesion** are terms which describe how texts, spoken or written, make sense and how parts of a text are joined together.

Coherence

Exercise 1

Read the text below. Does it make sense? Why or why not? Then read the next section.

On arriving at the station, come to the booking office to collect your tickets. London is only 50 minutes away by train! The train at platform 3 is for Cambridge. Why not visit our new transport museum or spend a day riding our city tour buses?

The text above does not make sense even though it is about one **topic** (transport) and there is **lexis** that relates to this topic (*station, booking office, tickets, train, platform, transport, buses*). It does not make sense because it is hard to see how the sentences relate to one another, it is probably unlike any text you are familiar with and the language does not all seem to belong to the same **text type**. The first sentence is like an email to a customer, the second is like a promotional advertisement for rail travel, the third is an announcement made at a train station and the final sentence is from a tourist leaflet. We use the term **coherent** to describe a text that makes sense because the ideas in it fit together clearly and logically. The text above lacks coherence.

Coherence is achieved when:

- a text follows the patterns you expect from one particular text type
- the topic can be identified and the text is consistently relevant to this topic
- the sentences clearly relate to one another and are organised logically
- the language used is consistently appropriate in **register**.

An example of a coherent text would be this email to a customer of a train company.

On arriving at the station, come to the booking office to collect your tickets. Please remember to bring your online receipt with you or some form of picture ID (for example, a passport or driver's licence). Once you have your tickets, check the departure boards to find out which platform your train departs from or speak to any of our staff who will be pleased to help you. Thank you for choosing Western Trains. We hope you enjoy your journey.

■ Cohesion

Exercise 2

Read the sentences/phrases below and put them in order.

When I arrived at the station   1
Next, I went to the platform
so I went to a café
the first thing I did was collect my tickets
and had a cup of coffee
but my train had been delayed

Check your answers on page 129 and then read the next section.

We use the term **cohesive** to describe a text in which the different parts are clearly linked. Cohesion is achieved by using grammar and lexis to join parts of the text together. For example, in Exercise 2, you probably used clues such as *the first thing*, *Next*, *but*, *so*, *café* and *coffee* to help you put the sentences and phrases in the correct order.

Coherence and cohesion are different things: a text that is cohesive is not necessarily coherent and vice versa. For example, in this note to a friend, the text is coherent but it is not obviously cohesive: *Arrived late. Bit noisy. Sorry.* However, a lack of cohesion can sometimes affect coherence. For example, in Exercise 1, there are no clues in the text about how these sentences are connected to one another.

■ Grammatical cohesion

In Exercise 2, the words and phrases *when, next, so, the first thing* and *but* are examples of grammatical cohesion. These particular words and phrases are sometimes called linkers because they link clauses, phrases and sentences together and show how they relate to each other. The linkers *when, but* and *so* are called **conjunctions** (see page 76, Unit 14).

Exercise 3

What relationship between the clauses and words is expressed by the underlined conjunctions below? For example, in <u>After</u> *I finished work, I went to the theatre, after* expresses a relationship of time between *I finished work* and *I went to the theatre*.

1 <u>When</u> I arrived, I met Joe <u>and</u> Sue <u>but</u> Sam wasn't there <u>because</u> she was ill.
2 <u>As soon as</u> you give us your credit card details, we can <u>either</u> post <u>or</u> email your tickets to you.

Check your answers on pages 129–30 and read the notes.

In Exercise 2, the linkers *the first thing* and *next* were used. These are both **adverbial** and show the order of the actions in a text. Other linkers that also do this are: *then, firstly, after that* and *finally*. Linkers can also be used for other purposes such as expressing results (e.g. *so, therefore, consequently*), contrasting (e.g. *instead, alternatively*) and summarising (e.g. *therefore, so*).

■ Reference

Exercise 4

Look at the underlined words in the sentences below. What does each refer to? Number 1 is done for you.

1 The train was late. <u>It</u> didn't arrive till eight!   *'It' refers to 'the train'.*
2 If John and Sue don't hurry, <u>they</u>'ll miss the train.
3 <u>It</u> was a long journey but we made it in the end.
4 <u>Here</u>'s the website address for times: www.traintimes.org
5 [*On a train*] Sorry, you'll have to move. <u>These</u> are reserved for people with children.
6 [*A printed sign in a station*] Trains to Brighton <u>this</u> way.

Check your answers on page 130.

If a word refers back to something earlier in a text, it is called an **anaphoric reference** (e.g. number 1 above). If it refers forward to something later in a text, it is called a **cataphoric reference** (e.g. number 3 above). If it refers to something that is not in the text itself, it is called an **exophoric reference** (e.g. number 5 above).

The most common words used for these different types of reference are:

● **pronouns** (e.g. *it, she, yours, this, that, these, those, some, who, where*)
● **determiners** (e.g. *a, the, this, that, these, those, her, his*)
● **adverbs** (e.g. *there, here, then*).

Exercise 5

Look at Exercise 4 again and identify the different types of reference in numbers 2, 4 and 6. What parts of speech are these words?

Check your answers on page 130.

■ Longer references and fixed phrases

Exercise 6

Look at the underlined words and phrases in the sentences below. What does each refer to? Is each one anaphoric or cataphoric?

1 We saw the sun coming up, <u>which</u> was nice. <u>It</u> was really lovely.
2 I once went to Italy on holiday but <u>that</u> was many years ago.
3 Listen carefully. <u>This</u> is very important. Don't touch the red or the black wires.
4 If your computer won't open this page, please try <u>the following</u>: sign in to your account again; reload this software; call our help desk.
5 She's very sociable and generous. <u>This is why</u> she's got so many friends.

Check your answers on page 130.

Words such as *which, it, that* and *this* can be used as anaphoric or cataphoric references to longer sections of text, for example numbers 1, 2 and 3 in Exercise 6. These longer sections of text may be phrases, sentences or much longer stretches. *It* is generally used to refer to topics that have already been introduced (e.g. number 1 in Exercise 6).

Some fixed phrases are used as references, for example number 4 (cataphoric) and 5 (anaphoric). Other examples of fixed phrases for cataphoric reference are *below* and *as follows*, while examples for anaphoric reference are *the former, the latter* and *the previous*.

■ Substitution and ellipsis

Exercise 7

Look at the sentences below. What do the underlined words in 2 and 3 replace? Which words have not been repeated in numbers 1 and 3?

1 A: Have you got any cash? B: No, I haven't.
2 I had a great time yesterday and I think Peter <u>did</u> too.
3 I've bought a shirt. A red <u>one</u>.

Now read the next section.

Substitution is when a word is used to replace another word, phrase or clause. It is used to avoid repetition in a text. In number 2 above, *did* is a substitute for *had a great time* and in number 3, *one* substitutes for *shirt*. Common words used for substitution are *do* and certain pronouns such as *another, any, both, all* and *none*.

Ellipsis is when a word or words are omitted from a sentence but not replaced with anything else. Words can be omitted because the context tells us that they could be there, for example *got any cash* in number 1 and *I've bought* in number 3.

■ Lexical cohesion

In Exercise 2, we saw that using the words *café* and *coffee* helped to link the parts of a text. Lexical cohesion involves the use of similar words or words in the same **lexical set** in one text. For example, *café* and *coffee* belong to the same lexical set. When two or more words from the same lexical set appear in a text, it is called a **lexical chain**. For example, in *The <u>reader</u> <u>read</u> a <u>text</u> <u>written</u> by a famous <u>author</u>*, all the underlined words are part of a lexical chain.

Lexical cohesion can also involve the repetition of words in a text either in the same form or in forms from the same **word family**. For example, in *I've lost my new <u>phone</u>, the lovely new <u>phone</u> I got last month* the same form is used. In *We've got a huge <u>collection</u> of paintings; we've been <u>collecting</u> them for years* the underlined words are from the same word family.

■ Parallelism

Exercise 8

Look at the sentences below. What is similar about the underlined parts in each?

1 In my job at the restaurant I have to <u>meet</u>, <u>greet</u> and <u>seat</u> people.
2 Her car's <u>better</u> and <u>faster</u>. However, mine's <u>cheaper</u> and <u>easier</u> to park.
3 The wind <u>was blowing</u> and the rain <u>was beating</u> against the windows.

Now read the next section to compare your ideas.

Parallelism is the term used to describe the repetition of a form in clauses or sentences. For example, in number 1 above, all the verbs are in the **base form**, in number 2 all the forms are **comparative adjectives** and are formed by adding the **suffix** -*er*, and in number 3 the **past continuous/progressive** is used twice. The repetition of the definite article + noun in number 3 is also an example of parallelism. In addition, parallelism can refer to repetition of sounds (*meet, greet, seat*) and **rhythm** (two syllables with the stress on the first syllable: *better, faster, cheaper*).

All of the features of cohesion in this unit (e.g. anaphoric reference, linkers, ellipsis, parallelism) are sometimes referred to as **cohesive devices**. It is cohesive devices such as these that give a text cohesion and can play a part in making it coherent.

FOLLOW-UP ACTIVITIES *(See page 130 for answers)*

1 Rewrite the sentences and utterances below using substitution and ellipsis.
   1 A: Do you like coffee and tea? B: Yes, I like coffee and tea.
   2 We know Clare well. You'll like Clare.
   3 John likes football and tennis but John doesn't play football and tennis well.
   4 I need a new pen and Sue needs a new pen too.

2 Identify how the underlined cohesive devices in the text below are used. For example, *This* [*substitution and anaphoric reference to the title* Check-in]. Can you find a lexical chain and examples of parallelism?

Check-in ——————————

<u>This</u> is an important part of <u>your</u> airport experience. <u>Firstly</u>, <u>because</u> <u>you</u> will meet <u>our</u> friendly staff, <u>who</u> can provide information about your flight, <u>and</u> <u>secondly</u> because you will be able to choose the seat you want. <u>For these reasons</u> you should arrive early at your terminal. <u>After</u> checking in, you should go to passport control.

DISCOVERY ACTIVITIES

1 Look at the section called 'Grammar across turns and sentences' (pages 242–65) in the *Cambridge Grammar of English* by Ronald Carter and Michael McCarthy, Cambridge University Press 2006. What words and phrases can be used to achieve cohesion and coherence? How do they help with cohesion and coherence? For example, are they used in anaphoric reference, in substitution, etc.?

2 Find a text and underline examples of linkers, conjunctions, substitutions, ellipsis, lexical chains and repetition. Are there any examples of parallelism?

TKT: KAL practice task 16 *(See page 133 for answers)*

A teacher is using an article from a newspaper to research cohesive devices.

For questions **1-6**, look at the types of cohesive device and choose the line (**A**, **B** or **C**) that contains an example.

Article from a newspaper

Bretton Park is to receive £200,000 to redevelop its play areas and gardens.	*line 1*
This huge amount of money was agreed last night by the Council, who have	*line 2*
been awarded funds to modernise leisure facilities in the area. 'Last night,	*line 3*
we discussed various strong options, though this project is easily the best,'	*line 4*
said Councillor Jo Bingley. She added, 'We hope to do the same for other	*line 5*
groups and organisations but can't until Bretton Park is completed.'	*line 6*

Types of cohesive device

1 lexical chain in the same line
   A line 1   **B** line 3   **C** line 4
2 substitution of a noun in the same line
   A line 2   **B** line 3   **C** line 6
3 an anaphoric reference to a proper noun
   A line 3   **B** line 5   **C** line 6
4 substitution of a verb in the same line
   A line 2   **B** line 4   **C** line 5
5 ellipsis of a verb
   A line 3   **B** line 4   **C** line 6
6 a conjunction showing contrast
   A line 1   **B** line 4   **C** line 5

Unit 17   Features of spoken discourse

LEARNING OUTCOME

KNOWLEDGE: how spoken and written text types differ and key terms associated with spoken discourse

■ Spoken and written discourse

A number of features are found in both written and spoken **discourse** such as reference, **substitution**, **ellipsis**, **conjunctions** and other **cohesive devices** (see Unit 16). Some spoken texts are more similar to written discourse than others and this depends on whether the spoken text is:

- planned and structured (e.g. a presentation at a business meeting)
- supported by writing (e.g. a lecture using notes)
- a monologue (one person speaking) or a **dialogue** (two or more people speaking to each other in an exchange, i.e. one person speaks and another responds to what they have said).

Generally speaking, if a spoken text is planned, or supported by writing, or is a monologue (e.g. in a lecture), it tends to be more similar to written discourse. The less planned and more interactional the spoken discourse is (e.g. in an **informal** conversation), the less it will have in common with written discourse. In this unit we will be looking particularly at the features of unplanned spoken discourse.

■ Features of spoken discourse

Exercise 1

Look at the text below and the one on page 94 and note the ways in which the spoken text differs from the written one. For example, the lexis in the spoken text is often simpler than the written one (*old* vs. *ancient*).

A hotel information leaflet

> Thank you for choosing the Grand Hotel and we would like to extend a warm welcome to you and your family. The hotel is situated in the ancient, historical centre of the city, with all the amenities and entertainment opportunities that this offers. If you would like further information on facilities in the vicinity, please do not hesitate to contact Reception. In addition, we have a dedicated television channel offering advice on all aspects of the hotel and our city. We sincerely hope that you enjoy your stay.

A conversation between two friends who have checked in to the Grand Hotel

A: So, here we are … how do … what do you think?

B: About the hotel or the …?

A: … The area … think it's OK?

B: Er … yeah, nice … old, nice old buildings and stuff and—

A: Lots of places to eat and bars …

B: Yeah … and museums …

A: … and clean …

B: Yeah …

A: … and not too busy … What time do they close? … the museums …

B: Call Reception …

A: OK. Yeah, I'll … [*picks up telephone*]

Now read the next section.

There are certain features that are more common in spoken discourse, particularly in conversation, than in written discourse. These include:

- shorter, simpler sentences. For example: *Call Reception* vs. *If you would like further information on facilities in the vicinity, please do not hesitate to contact Reception.*
- simpler **lexis**. For example: *old* vs. *ancient, historical; area* vs. *vicinity.*
- simpler grammar. For example: *here we are* vs. *we would like to extend a warm welcome to.*
- 'incorrect' grammar. For example: [*Do you*] *think it's OK?* (This looks like 'incorrect' grammar because of the ellipsis.)
- simpler conjunctions and linkers. For example: *and* vs. *in addition to*
- interruptions. For example: B: *stuff and—* A: *Lots of places to eat*
- incomplete **utterances**. For example: *OK. Yeah, I'll …*
- pauses, which are shown above as: …
- **hesitations**, such as the gaps in the conversation above. Repetition is another way of hesitating; for example: *nice … old, nice old.*
- fillers. For example, the sound *er* is called a filler because it fills a pause while the speaker thinks of what to say next.
- **repair strategies**. For example: *About the hotel or the …?; … the museums … .* These often involve things such as asking for or giving clarification or self-correction. They keep the conversation going when there is a chance that it will stop or when it has already stopped due to misunderstanding. Repair strategies often correct or change what someone has said.
- vague language. For example: *stuff, places to eat.* These words and phrases refer to things in general rather than to specific things.
- false starts. For example: *how do … .* The speaker starts speaking, changes their mind about what to say, and then begins again.

In addition to the points above, the **register** is typical of this **text type** (i.e. a conversation between friends). For example, the use of language is informal compared to the written text, which is significantly more **formal**. (For more on the register of spoken and written discourse, see pages 84–5, Unit 15.)

■ Opening and closing, turn-taking and back-channelling

> **Exercise 2**
> Look at the extract below from the conversation in Exercise 1. How do the underlined parts help the progress of the conversation? For example, *So* helps start the conversation.
>
> *line 1* A: <u>So</u>, here we are … how do … <u>what do you think?</u>
> *line 2* B: About the hotel <u>or the …?</u>
> *line 3* A: … The area … <u>think it's OK?</u>
> *line 4* B: Er … yeah, nice … old, nice old buildings and stuff and—
> *line 5* A: Lots of places to eat and bars …
> *line 6* B: <u>Yeah</u> … and museums …
> *line 7* A: … and clean …
>
> Check your answers on pages 130–1 and read the notes. Then read the next section.

Opening and closing a conversation are two types of discourse function. To open a conversation in English, it is common to use general questions (e.g. *How's it going?*) or words such as *so*, *well* and *anyway*. Similarly, to close a conversation in English, words such as *well* and phrases such as *it's been lovely talking …* are often used. Words such as *so*, *well* and *anyway* are called **discourse markers** because they tell the listener (or reader) what is going to happen in the discourse. (For more information on discourse markers, see pages 100–1, Unit 18.) In order to help you decide what the discourse function of a word or phrase is in a text, look at the **context** and the surrounding language.

Another type of discourse function is **turn-taking**. This is the act of speaking and then listening to another speaker in sequence. Conversations are made up of a series of turns, and there are various ways of showing another person that your turn is finishing or that their turn should begin. For example, in lines 1, 2 and 3, questions are used to invite the other person to speak. The same is true of pauses, for example in line 7 A knows it is OK to speak because B has previously paused. **Intonation** also helps with turn-taking. For example, when you hear a speaker's intonation fall at the end of a sentence, it is often a signal that you can speak. (For more information on intonation, see Unit 8.)

In line 6, the word *Yeah* is used to show A that B is listening to what he is saying. This use of words such as *yeah, right, really?*, and sounds such as *uh-huh* and *mmm*, is called **back-channelling** and often has the discourse function of showing that you are interested, sympathetic or simply that you understand.

■ Adaptation to audience

> **Exercise 3**
>
> Look at the dialogue below. How does A's language change from his first utterance to his second? Why do you think it changes?
>
> A: Hi ... how's things?
> B: I'm sorry ... do I know you?
> A: Oh, I do apologise. I thought you were John ... I mean, I thought you were a friend.
>
> Now read the next section.

A speaker's use of language changes depending on the person they are speaking to: their audience. In the dialogue above, A's use of grammar and lexis changes register and becomes more formal because he realises that B is a stranger. In the same way, an adult will speak differently to a child than to another adult, a doctor will use different medical lexis when speaking to a patient than she would when speaking to another doctor.

In A's final utterance, he changes *John* to *a friend* because he needs to clarify *John* for B (a stranger). He is using a repair strategy. The act of saying the same thing but in different words more appropriate to the context, is often referred to as **reformulation**. Discourse markers such as *I mean* can be used to introduce a reformulation.

Another way we can adapt our language to our audience is to **paraphrase** (use different words to express the meaning of another word or phrase, often to make its meaning clearer). An example of paraphrasing is in the dialogue below:

In a car mechanic's workshop
A: I'm afraid your fuel injectors have gone.
B: I'm sorry?
A: The part that pushes the petrol into the engine.
B: I see. Is that expensive?

B has a better understanding at the end of the dialogue because A has paraphrased the problem words *fuel injectors*. **Summarising**, on the other hand, is when you restate the message of a text but in fewer words. Discourse markers such as *to put it another way*, *what I mean is*, *so* and *to sum up* are used to introduce a paraphrase or a summary.

FOLLOW-UP ACTIVITIES *(See page 131 for answers)*

1 Match the terms on the left with the definitions on the right.

1 turn-taking	a) Using different words to express the meaning of other words or phrases.
2 back-channelling	b) A word or sound used while the speaker thinks of what to say next.
3 paraphrasing	c) Using words and sounds to show that you are listening.
4 filler	d) One person makes an utterance, followed by another person.

2 Use the context and surrounding language in the conversation below to identify the discourse functions of the underlined parts.

Sue: Hi. <u>How's it going?</u>

John: I've got a bit of a headache …

Sue: <u>Oh dear</u> …

John: … and I think I've got a chest infection.

Sue: <u>Poor you</u> … you should see the doctor.

John: Yes, I've got an appointment tomorrow but my car's not working …

Sue: <u>Er</u> … <u>well</u>, I could probably drive you there.

John: Good … <u>I mean</u>, that's very kind, thank you.

Sue: No problem … <u>Anyway</u>, <u>sorry</u>, but I really need to go.

DISCOVERY ACTIVITIES

1 Find a spoken text (e.g. a recording or a transcript of a dialogue in an English-language coursebook). Note the features that are typical of spoken discourse.

2 Look at the English language coursebooks that you or your colleagues use. What aspects of spoken discourse do they include? Are there any that you would add?

TKT: KAL practice task 17 (*See page 133 for answers*)

A teacher is using a dialogue to research features of spoken discourse.

For questions **1-5**, look at the underlined examples in the dialogue and match them with the features of spoken discourse listed **A**, **B** and **C**.

You will need to use some options more than once.

Features of spoken discourse

> **A** back-channelling
> **B** false start
> **C** conversational repair

Dialogue

Tom: Er … excuse me …

Sue: **1** <u>What can</u> … how can I help?

Tom: **2** <u>I was wondering if you</u> … could you tell me where …

Sue: **3** <u>Mmm?</u>

Tom: … the nearest shop is? **4** <u>I mean</u> supermarket.

Sue: Oh, er … yes, just go right here …

Tom: **5** <u>OK, yes.</u>

Unit 18   Semantic and pragmatic meanings

LEARNING OUTCOMES

KNOWLEDGE:
- how semantic and pragmatic meanings differ
- different discourse markers and how they function in discourse

■ What are semantic and pragmatic meanings?

Look at the sentences and word below and the descriptions of their meaning.

Sentence	Description of meaning
1 I can open the window.	I am able to open (not close) the window (not the door).
2 It's very warm in here.	It isn't cold in here.
3 Is the flight booked?	I'm asking if the flight is reserved.
4 Is your brother in?	I'm asking if your brother (not your sister) is in the house where he lives.
5 Thank you for not smoking.	I'm grateful to you for not smoking.
6 Silence	No noise

The **literal meaning** of the sentences and words above is sometimes referred to as their **semantic meaning** and sometimes you only need to understand semantic meaning to understand a sentence, **utterance** or a word. However, the semantic meaning is not always the speaker's or writer's intention; it is not this that they want the listener or reader to understand.

Exercise 1
Look at the situations and dialogues below. Does the meaning of the underlined sentences and words in the table above change now you can see them in context?

1 *Two strangers in a hot waiting room*
   A: <u>I can open the window.</u>
   B: That would be very kind. Thank you.
2 *A couple at home*
   A: <u>It's very warm in here.</u>
   B: I'll turn the air-con up.
3 *A couple needing a holiday*
   A: <u>Is the flight booked?</u>
   B: Leave me alone! You know how busy I've been.

4 *On the phone*
A: Is your brother in?
B: I'll just get him.
5 *A notice in a taxi*
Thank you for not smoking.
6 *A notice in a library*
Silence

Check your answers on page 131.

The meaning given to a piece of language by the **context** and situation in which it is said or written is called the **pragmatic meaning**. For example, the pragmatic meaning of number 1 above is *I'm offering to open the window because it's hot in here and I can see that you're uncomfortable*. Similarly, number 5 is not really saying *Thank you*; it means *Please don't smoke* or *You aren't allowed to smoke*.

As well as having semantic and pragmatic meanings, pieces of language have different **functions**. For example, the function of number 1 above is making an offer and that of number 5 is expressing prohibition. The function of a piece of language can vary depending on the context in which it is used. For example, *Shall I help you with that?* usually expresses an offer but it could also express a criticism if the speaker does not think the listener is doing something well.

Exercise 2

Look at the dialogues below. What is the pragmatic meaning and the function of each of the underlined utterance? Use the context to help you.

Dialogue 1

A: Are you a chicken man?
B: I am, yes.
A: OK. I'll get some for dinner.

Dialogue 2

A: Do you know what the time is?
B: Sorry. I got held up at work.
A: I wish you'd think about me more.

Check your answers on page 131.

If you understood the pragmatic meaning of the underlined sentences in the dialogues above, it was because you were able to understand the context correctly. This is very important when interpreting pragmatic meaning. Now look at the different response (underlined) in Dialogue 2 below:

A: Do you know what the time is?
B: Ten thirty.
A: I … you … er …

B answers A's question literally because he/she does not understand that it is a **rhetorical question** (a question that does not require an answer) showing A is angry. B may not understand this because he/she does not understand the context but it will also probably be because B does not understand the way A's utterance is said. A would probably convey their anger through pitch and **intonation**, as well as gesture. As a result of the misunderstanding, A does not know how to continue the dialogue.

So, when interpreting the pragmatic meaning of language, you need to pay attention to the manner in which it is said (pitch, intonation, gesture, facial expression, etc.) and to the context in which it is said. The latter includes:

- who is speaking/writing
- why they are speaking/writing
- who they are speaking to/writing for
- the relationship between the speaker and listener or the writer and reader
- what is normal or acceptable in their social group or culture. For example, in Dialogue 2, it seems to be unacceptable to get home at ten thirty.

If any of the above points are not understood, there might be a communication breakdown: the communication would stop working.

■ Discourse markers

Discourse markers are words and phrases with the general function of telling the listener/reader what to expect from the text that follows. For example, they tell us if the **topic** will change direction (e.g. *anyway*) or if the following text is a summary (e.g. *to summarise*, *then*). They are also used to add the speaker's/writer's view of what will be, or has just been, said. Linkers are sometimes included in this category. (For more information on linkers, see page 88, Unit 16.)

Exercise 3
Look at the extracts below from a dialogue and a written text. What is the specific function of the underlined discourse markers?

Extract 1
A: <u>OK</u> … what I'm going to tell you …
B: Mmm?
A: … is really relevant to us, <u>in fact</u> …
B: OK.
A: … <u>I mean</u>, important for both of us.
B: Oh! … <u>So</u>, just us or John, too?

Extract 2

Dear Jane
Here we are in the sunny south! <u>Frankly</u>, the journey wasn't good but, <u>amazingly</u>, we all got here. <u>Apparently</u>, the check-in staff tried to move people from our flight to a later one and people were shouting at them but, <u>actually</u>, it wasn't their fault. It was the airline and their systems. <u>Anyway</u>, I'll never book with them again, <u>obviously</u>. <u>By the way</u>, did you manage to book anything? <u>Unfortunately</u>, this place is full but …

Check your answers on pages 131–2. Other discourse markers that perform the same functions are given there.

It is more common for discourse markers to appear before the text they refer to (e.g. *unfortunately*) but they can also appear elsewhere in a sentence (e.g. *obviously*). They are normally separated from the rest of a written text by commas. Discourse markers are often **adverb** forms (e.g. *unfortunately*), short **clauses** (e.g. *I mean*) or phrases with a **preposition** (e.g. *in fact*).

Some discourse markers are more common in spoken texts (e.g. *right, OK*), others are more common in written texts (e.g. *in summary*) and others can be used in both (e.g. all of the markers in the written text above). Some discourse markers are more **formal** than others, for example *moving on to another topic* (formal) vs. *by the way* (**informal**). Some can be used to show the attitude of the speaker or writer (e.g. *amazingly*) and others predict the type of text that follows (e.g. *In other words* can be used to introduce a clarification).

FOLLOW-UP ACTIVITIES *(See page 132 for answers)*

1 Match the utterances on the left with a possible pragmatic meaning on the right.

   1 Is that the best you can do?   a) I really want to leave now.
   2 Do you have to go?   b) I'm not very hungry.
   3 That's a big piece.   c) I'd love you to stay.
   4 It's very late.   d) I don't think your effort is good enough.

2 What are the functions of the underlined discourse markers in the text below? Which ones express the writer's attitude?

> I started buying lottery tickets a couple of years ago and, <u>amazingly</u>, I won with my fourth ticket. It was completely unexpected <u>of course</u> because the chances are very small, <u>obviously</u>. People told me I'd change but <u>in fact</u> I really didn't change at all. <u>Sadly</u>, other people thought I had and I lost a lot of friends.

DISCOVERY ACTIVITIES

1 Look at the section on discourse markers in *Grammar for English Language Teachers (Second Edition)* by Martin Parrott, Cambridge University Press 2010. How many additional markers does he add to those in this unit?

2 Find a written text and a spoken text (e.g. a recording of a dialogue, or a written transcript of a recording). Underline (or write down, if it is a recording) all the discourse markers you can find in the texts. Use the context of the texts to decide on the function of the discourse markers.

....

TKT: KAL practice task 18 *(See page 133 for answers)*

A teacher is writing a worksheet on discourse markers for her class.

For questions **1-5**, match the example sentences with the types of discourse marker listed **A-C**.

You will need to use some options more than once.

_____

Types of discourse marker

> **A** an adverb used as a discourse marker
> **B** a prepositional phrase used as a discourse marker
> **C** a discourse marker that expresses the speaker's attitude

Example sentences

1 So, what shall we do this evening?
2 I know what you mean, but, in reality, it's not like that.
3 The newspapers don't think it's true, actually.
4 To be honest, I'm afraid, I can't help you.
5 When we discussed it calmly, I think we agreed, on the whole.

....

A sample answer sheet is on page 114.

A teacher is researching different ways of describing vocabulary.

For questions **1-8**, match the sets of words and phrases with the terms that describe them listed **A-I**.

Mark the correct letter (**A-I**) on your answer sheet.

There is one extra option you do not need to use.

Terms

A	compound adjectives
B	compound nouns
C	word families
D	synonyms
E	verb–noun collocations
F	homophones
G	antonyms
H	adjective–noun collocations
I	homonyms

Sets of words and phrases

1 prepared (adjective) – preparation (noun); advertise (verb) – advertisement (noun)

2 give – take; light – dark

3 strong opinion; heavy accent

4 have faith – trust; work – labour

5 slow-moving; well-spoken

6 threw – through; bare – bear

7 car park; housework

8 light (noun) – light (adjective); rose (noun) – rose (verb)

A teacher is correcting the use of affixation in his students' homework and is writing comments on the mistakes they have made.

For questions **9-13**, match the teacher's comments with the students' mistakes listed **A-F**.

Mark the correct letter (**A-F**) on your answer sheet.

There is one extra option you do not need to use.

Mistakes the students made

A	The problem was it was totally unbelieveable.
B	We left at the begining of June.
C	They hoped it would be completely inaffected, but it wasn't.
D	It was the most important achievment of the last century in my opinion.
E	His grammar is a little inaccurately.
F	I found the explanation they gave completely unecessary.

Teacher's comments

9 Be careful. When you add prefixes, letters are not normally added or taken away.

10 Double the final consonant of a word when adding a suffix starting with a vowel.

11 You should drop the *e* here because the suffix begins with a vowel.

12 Remember, if a word ends in *e,* you don't need to drop it if you add a suffix starting with a consonant.

13 Good. Your prefix is right but this suffix is used for adverbs, not adjectives.

A teacher is doing research on lexis and is using an email he received from a friend to provide examples of different types of lexis.

For questions **14-20**, look at the email. Read the questions about different kinds of form and meaning in lexis and the three possible answers listed **A**, **B** and **C**.

Choose the correct answer.

Mark the correct letter (**A**, **B** or **C**) on your answer sheet.

Email

Hey Johnny	
How's it going over there in Ireland? What have you been doing? I was just	line 1
thinking about you and thought I'd send a message to see how things are.	line 2
I've just come to south London. I didn't like my old flat and prefer the new	line 3
one – it's a space issue. Loads of room to have you to stay any time. So, get	line 4
yourself onto a plane and over here, mate. Flying's not expensive if you look	line 5
online and fly Thursday at 5.00 a.m. Are you an early bird (ha, ha)? It'd be	line 6
so cool to see you. Give me a call. I'm around most evenings. See you.	line 7

14 Which line in the text contains a compound preposition?
   A line 1   **B** line 3   **C** line 5

15 Which line in the text contains an adjective made with a suffix?
   A line 2   **B** line 5   **C** line 6

16 Which line in the text contains a phrase with figurative meaning?
   A line 3   **B** line 4   **C** line 6

17 Which line in the text contains two synonyms in the same line?
   A line 2   **B** line 4   **C** line 5

18 Which line in the text contains a verb–preposition collocation?
   A line 2   **B** line 3   **C** line 7

19 Which line in the text contains two contractions in the same line?
   A line 1   **B** line 3   **C** line 7

20 Which line in the text contains two words in the same lexical set in the same line?
   A line 1   **B** line 5   **C** line 7

A teacher is listening to a recorded conversation to find examples of features of connected speech to use in a lesson.

For questions **21-29,** match the phonemic transcriptions on parts of the recording with the features of connected speech they exemplify listed **A-D**.

Mark the correct letter (**A**, **B**, **C** or **D**) on your answer sheet.

You need to use some options more than once.

Features of connected speech

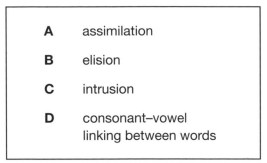

A	assimilation
B	elision
C	intrusion
D	consonant–vowel linking between words

Phonemic transcriptions

/laɪkɪt/
21 So, how did you like it then, the break?

/ðɪʃjɪə/
22 Good, good. Better this year, definitely.

/wɒzɪt/
23 Was it North America you went to?

/kænədərənd/
24 Yeah. We went to Canada and had a great time.

/mʌsgəʊ/
25 I really must go there some time.

/jerɪt/
26 Yeah, it is really brilliant.

/wɔːkɪŋɪnðə/
27 We went walking in the south of Spain.

/lʌvlɪjənd/
28 Lovely and hot, I bet. When did you get back?

/lɑːsætədɪ/
29 Last Saturday. Just long enough, I think.

A teacher is giving her students advice on how to pronounce consonant sounds.

For questions **30-35**, look at the advice the teacher gives and choose the sound (**A, B** or **C**) she is referring to.

Mark the correct letter (**A, B** or **C**) on your answer sheet.

---

30 You need to put your tongue between your teeth.
    A /ʃ/   **B** /θ/   **C** /d/

31 You need to use your voice.
    A /ð/   **B** /s/   **C** /f/

32 You need to put your lips together.
    A /d/   **B** /ŋ/   **C** /p/

33 You need to touch your bottom lip with your top teeth.
    A /n/   **B** /v/   **C** /θ/

34 You need to keep your lips together.
    A /m/   **B** /uː/   **C** /w/

35 You <u>don't</u> need to use your voice.
    A /dʒ/   **B** /v/   **C** /tʃ/

A teacher is writing an exercise on verb forms for her students and is using an extract from a story to find examples.

For questions **36-44**, look at the extract. Read the questions about verb forms and the three possible answers, **A**, **B** or **C**.

Choose the correct answer.

Mark the correct letter (**A**, **B** or **C**) on your answer sheet.

Having arrived late at the farm, Susan wasn't sure whether her hosts would   *line 1*
be able to provide her with any food and didn't ask immediately because it   *line 2*
wasn't polite. However, once she had unpacked her bags, she made her way   *line 3*
down to the kitchen to find Mr or Mrs Johnson. They weren't on the ground   *line 4*
floor and, unsure of what else to do, she decided to make herself something   *line 5*
to eat. She would have liked a full meal, despite the fact that it was getting   *line 6*
very late, but there was only bread on the table. 'Not good,' she thought. It   *line 7*
was odd and she couldn't help wondering if the Johnsons had ever had   *line 8*
guests staying with them before. She was just cutting a thick slice of the   *line 9*
bread when a voice behind her asked what she thought she was doing.   *line 10*

36 Which line in the text contains a past simple negative auxiliary?
    A line 1   **B** line 2   **C** line 4

37 Which line in the text contains a past modal structure?
    A line 2   **B** line 6   **C** line 8

38 Which line in the text contains the past perfect simple?
    A line 1   **B** line 6   **C** line 8

39 Which line in the text contains the verb *to be* used as a main verb?
    A line 4   **B** line 6   **C** line 10

40 Which line in the text contains reported speech?
    A line 2   **B** line 7   **C** line 10

41 Which line in the text contains the past continuous describing an interrupted action?
    A line 6   **B** line 8   **C** line 9

42 Which line in the text contains the verb *to have* used as a main verb?
    A line 1   **B** line 6   **C** line 8

43 Which line in the text contains two non-finite verb forms?
    A line 3   **B** line 5   **C** line 7

44 Which line in the text contains the past continuous describing a developing situation?
    A line 1   **B** line 6   **C** line 10

A teacher is writing a worksheet on different patterns that follow reporting verbs.

For questions **45-50**, look at the reporting verbs and the three patterns. Two of the patterns can follow the reporting verb. One of the patterns **CANNOT** follow the reporting verb.

Mark the option (**A**, **B** or **C**) which **CANNOT** follow each verb.

---

45 warn

    A + direct object + to + infinitive
    B + direct object + that + clause
    C + to infinitive + indirect object

46 advise

    A + base form
    B + *ing* form
    C + direct object + to + infinitive

47 demand

    A + that + clause
    B + direct object + to + infinitive
    C + to + infinitive

48 admit

    A + to + infinitive
    B + *ing* form
    C + that + clause

49 promise

    A + that + clause
    B + *ing* form
    C + to + infinitive

50 tell

    A + direct object + to + infinitive
    B + that + clause
    C + direct object + about + *ing* form

A teacher is writing a worksheet on different uses of *-ing* forms for her students.

For questions **51-58**, match the uses of *-ing* forms with the examples listed **A-I**.

Mark the correct letter (**A-I**) on your answer sheet.

There is one extra option you do not need to use.

Examples

A	Have you been living here long?	
B	How long will you have been studying here by then?	
C	It wasn't that he hadn't been trying to leave.	
D	He must have been working.	
E	It's very interesting you should say that.	
F	Won't you be staying at home?	
G	Is that where you're living next month?	
H	Look! It's started raining again. I wish it wouldn't.	
I	It's good travelling but getting home is nicer, I think.	

Uses of *-ing* forms

51 in the present continuous

52 as an adjective

53 in the future continuous

54 in the present perfect continuous

55 in the future perfect continuous

56 as a noun

57 in the past perfect continuous

58 as a pattern following a main verb

A teacher is preparing a worksheet on different types of clause.

For questions **59-65**, match the underlined examples of clauses with the types of clause listed **A**, **B** and **C**.

Mark the correct letter (**A**, **B** or **C**) on your answer sheet.

You need to use some options more than once.

Types of clause

A	a relative clause	
B	a main clause as part of a conditional	
C	a subordinate clause as part of a conditional	

Examples of clauses

59 | I might consider helping you <u>when you ask me nicely</u>.

60 | I'm trying to imagine it. Was it like the time <u>when you stayed with us</u>?

61 | <u>It's all a bit funny</u>, if you ask me.

62 | So, you're the woman <u>Tom told me about</u>!

63 | I'm not going <u>unless you come with me</u>.

64 | <u>Which might you prefer</u>, given the choice?

65 | Do you understand the reason <u>why I'm telling you this</u>?

A teacher is doing some research into the use of referencing in discourse and is looking for examples in an instruction leaflet.

For questions **66-74**, match the underlined examples in the instruction leaflet with the different types of referencing listed **A**, **B** and **C**.

Mark the correct letter (**A**, **B** or **C**) on your answer sheet.

You need to use some options more than once.

Different types of referencing

A	anaphoric reference
B	cataphoric reference
C	exophoric reference

Examples in the instruction leaflet

Dear Valued Customer,

66 I hope you are happy with this product. 67 It is important that you make sure 68 this washing machine is installed by one of the dependable organisations on the list below. 69 This will reduce the chances of problems in the future. But just in case 70 you have 71 any, 72 here's a number to call: 0800 5690 1234. The staff will help you find a solution and if they can't do 73 so – and 74 this is a promise – you'll get a new machine absolutely free. Enjoy your new machine!

A teacher is writing a test on different features of discourse.

For questions **75-80**, match the examples with the different features of discourse listed **A**, **B** and **C**.

Mark the correct letter (**A**, **B** or **C**) on your answer sheet.

You need to use some options more than once.

Different features of discourse

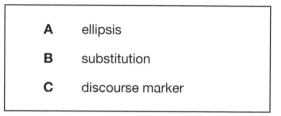

A	ellipsis
B	substitution
C	discourse marker

Examples

75 Is this the car you wanted – the blue one?

76 I don't like that restaurant and I know you don't!

77 I'm not keen on leaving the kids at home alone, to be honest.

78 The first thing is to sort out our summer holiday.

79 I loved that place and you did too, didn't you?

80 I've got a new car! A lovely new car!

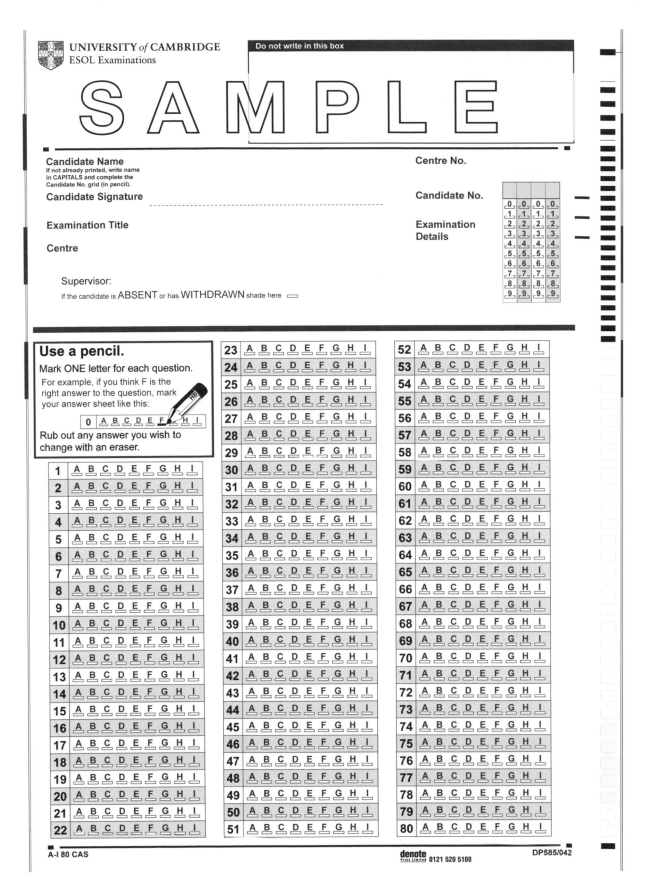

Exam tips for the TKT: KAL

- The TKT: KAL consists of one module which can be taken as an extension of the TKT Modules 1, 2 and 3 or on its own.
- The TKT: KAL has 80 questions altogether.
- There are four sections in the test:
  1 Lexis (20 questions)
  2 Phonology (15 questions)
  3 Grammar (30 questions)
  4 Discourse (15 questions)
- The task types in the test are: matching; multiple choice; finding the odd one out.
- The test lasts 80 minutes.

Before the exam

1 Know and understand the necessary TKT: KAL concepts and terms. Read the units in this book and do the Exercises, Follow-up activities, Discovery activities and TKT practice task in each unit.
2 Look at the list of terms in this book and in the *TKT Glossary* at http://www.cambridgeesol.org/exams/teaching-awards/tkt.html
3 Do a TKT: KAL practice test to become more familiar with the types of task and the content of the test.

During the exam

1 Quickly look at the different parts of the test to get an idea of the content.
2 Start the test at question 1 and work through to question 80. If you don't know an answer, make a mark on the exam paper and return to it later.
3 Read the instructions and questions very carefully to make sure you understand exactly what to do.
4 Make sure you shade the boxes (e.g. A, B, C, D) on the answer sheet with a pencil. Look at the sample answer sheet on page 114.
5 Be careful with matching questions which have options which you do not need to use or options that you need to use more than once.
6 Be particularly careful with odd-one-out questions in which you have to choose the answer that is **NOT** correct. (See page 109 for an example.)
7 Don't spend too long on one answer; all the questions have one mark.
8 Leave a few minutes at the end of the exam to check your answers. You will be told when you have ten minutes left.
9 Don't forget to put all your answers on the answer sheet.

Answer key for Exercises and Follow-up activities

UNIT 1
Exercise 2

1 *Table* has a different denotation here. It means 'an arrangement of facts and numbers in rows or blocks'. The connotation remains neutral.
2 The denotation has not changed: 'to stop doing something'. However, because the tense has changed the meaning is now 'past' (*gave*). Grammatical meaning such as this is part of the full meaning of a word.
3 The denotation has changed and *take* has 'lost' its original meaning. It now means 'travel by' but cannot be separated from *bus*.
4 The denotation has not changed but the connotation has become positive.

Exercise 3

Words/sets of words	Literal meaning	Figurative meaning
1 I ate so much I thought I was going to <u>burst</u>.	Explode like a balloon.	I felt extremely full.
2 She has <u>the voice of an angel</u>.	A voice like an angel's voice.	She speaks or sings beautifully.
3 He has such <u>a sunny smile</u>.	A smile like the sun.	A happy, positive, attractive smile.
4 We were <u>baking</u>. The weather was so hot	Cooking in the oven, like bread.	Extremely hot.

All the examples above are exaggerating the meaning the speakers want to express and this is a very common use of figurative language.

Follow-up activity 1

Item of lexis	Figurative? Meaning?	Register
1 Last Sunday was <u>boiling</u> hot!	Yes. Here it means very, very hot.	Informal with this meaning.
2 I <u>would appreciate it if you could</u> ...	No.	Formal

Item of lexis	Figurative? Meaning?	Register
3 Overwork can lead to serious <u>fatigue</u>.	No.	Used by people in the medical profession.
4 So, <u>how's it going</u>?	No (but *going* doesn't have a literal meaning here).	Informal.
5 See you soon. <u>Tons of love</u>, Anne	Yes. Here *tons* means *lots* rather than a weight.	Informal.

Follow-up activity 2

1 a) Literal meaning of 'take something from a surface and lift it'.
   b) A figurative meaning of 'collect me'.
2 a) A long thin piece of potato that is fried and usually eaten hot (from the *Cambridge Advanced Learner's Dictionary (Third Edition)*).
   b) A very small piece of computer equipment that contains electronic circuits. The register has changed the meaning. This definition of *chip* in the *Cambridge Advanced Learner's Dictionary (Third Edition)* includes the word 'SPECIALIZED'. This tells you that the word is used in particular contexts and often by particular people.
3 a) The literal meaning of 'travel to a place'.
   b) The figurative meaning of 'became'. Used as part of the collocation with *mad*.

UNIT 2
Exercise 2

1 *Furniture* is the heading of this category and *table*, *chair*, *sofa* and *bed* are all words in the category.
2 *Vegetable* is the heading of this category and *potato*, *carrot*, *cabbage* and *bean* are all words in the category.

Exercise 3
1 superordinate: animal; hyponym: horse
2 superordinate: clothes; hyponyms: dresses, trousers
3 superordinate: road vehicle; hyponym: car
4 superordinate: container; hyponyms: box, bottle

Exercise 4
1 flat / flat Both sound the same and are spelt the same. They have different meanings.
2 sea / see Both sound the same. They are spelt differently. They have different meanings.
3 close (verb) / close (adjective) Both are spelt the same. They have different sounds, i.e. *close* (verb) /kləʊz/ and *close* (adjective) /kləʊs/. They have different meanings.

Exercise 5
The words in numbers 1 and 3 have the same or a similar meaning to the other words while in numbers 2, 4 and 5 they have opposite or near opposite meanings.

Follow-up activity 1
1 A lexical set with the topic of vehicles/transport/getting to work, etc. They are hyponyms of *transport/vehicles*.
2 *Fruit* is the superordinate of the other three words. *Apple*, *orange* and *strawberry* are hyponyms of *fruit*.
3 Synonyms. Some have a stronger meaning, e.g. *love* and *adore*. *Adore* is often used in a more formal register whereas *be keen on* is often more informal. *Like* and *love* normally have a neutral register.
4 Homophones.
5 Antonyms. The first two are true antonyms. With *give/take*, one does not replace the other as an opposite. That is, the 'opposite' of *I give* is *I don't give* not *I take*.
6 *Cloudy*, *stupid* and *dark* are antonyms of *bright* but *bright* has changed its meaning in each case.

Follow-up activity 2
1 end
2 watch TV; see a film; go out for dinner. Topic = things to do at the weekend
3 sport
4 house
5 eye
6 little. This is a true antonym.

UNIT 3
Exercise 1
1 Three: *un + attract + ive*
   Un and *ive* are bound morphemes; *attract* is a free morpheme.
2 Two: *mid + day*
   Mid is a bound morpheme; *day* is a free morpheme.
3 Two: *move + ment*
   Move is a free morpheme; *ment* is a bound morpheme.
4 Three: *teach + er + s*
   Teach is a free morpheme; *er* and *s* are bound morphemes.

Exercise 2
1 *Un* changes the meaning of *attractive* to the opposite of *attractive*; *-ive* changes the verb *attract* into an adjective.
2 *Mid* adds the meaning of *in the middle of* to the word *day*.
3 *Ment* changes the verb *move* into a noun.
4 *Er* shows us that this word is a noun, i.e. it changes the part of speech from a verb to a noun; *s* shows us that it is plural.

Exercise 3

Verb	Noun	Adjective	Negative prefix + adjective
employ	employee employment employer	employed employable	unemployed unemployable
no verb. We use *to be possible*.	possibility	possible	impossible
depend	dependant	dependent dependable	independent
economise	economy economics	economic(al)	uneconomic(al)
record (Note, the stress is on the second syllable.)	record (Note, the stress is on the first syllable.)	recordable recorded record	non-recordable unrecorded

Exercise 4

1 The *y* has been changed to *i* (because when a suffix is added to a word ending in a consonant + *y*, the *y* normally changes to *i*).
2 The *e* has been dropped (because the suffix begins with a vowel).
3 The *e* has not been dropped (because the suffix begins with a consonant).

Exercise 5

Verb	Noun	Adjective	Negative prefix + adjective
1 believe	believer belief	believable	unbelievable
2 create	creation creator	creative	uncreative

Exercise 6

	Number of words
1 ice cream	1 or 2 (see below)
2 nice-looking	1 or 2 (see below)
3 dry clean	1 or 2 (see below)
4 homework	1 or 2 (see below)

Combining words (compounding) to make new words (compounds) is very common in English. All the compounds in the table above are made by combining two words. The new word is regarded as having one unit of meaning, which is different from the meanings of the words that make it. It is sometimes regarded as a single word. So, the answers in the second column above could be '1' or '2'. Notice that compounds can be written as one single word, as two separate words or by joining the two words with a hyphen. At times, a compound can be written in different ways; for example, *ice cream* may sometimes be written with a hyphen. How a compound is written is sometimes because of personal choice and sometimes because of generally accepted forms. For example, *homework* is always written as one word but in *dry clean* you can choose to use a hyphen or not. A dictionary will provide you with this information.

Exercise 7

1 *was not*. Some people see *wasn't* as a single word while others see it as two. The apostrophe replaces the letters that have been missed out.
2 *Digital Versatile Disc* or *Digital Video Disc*. Many abbreviations like this have completely replaced their full forms in English. They are used commonly when the full form is perhaps too 'technical' or too long to be easily remembered and/or used by the general public, e.g. CD (*compact disc*).
3 *advertisement*. *Advert* is often shortened even more to *ad*. It is very common in English to shorten words with a lot of syllables to make them easier and faster to say or write.
4 *Random Access Memory* (a computer term). It is pronounced as 'ram'.

Follow-up activity 1

1 inter – ent
2 under – er
3 un – ive
4 dis – ment

Follow-up activity 2

1 interpersonal (inter – al)
2 swimmer (-er)
3 car park
4 socialise

UNIT 4
Exercise 1
heavy: snow
strong: wind; sunshine
light: wind; snow
Heavy and *strong* have very similar meanings but they cannot always be used with the same nouns. For example, *heavy* commonly combines with *snow* but not with *wind* and *sunshine*. *Light* has the opposite meaning of *heavy* and *strong* in this context.

Exercise 2
go: home; mad
go home = travel home; go mad = become mad
catch: a bus; a ball
catch a bus = get on a bus; catch a ball = receive a ball which is thrown in your hand
take: a pill; a bus
take a pill = swallow a pill; take a bus = travel on a bus

Exercise 3

> I was in the supermarket the other day when this man <u>caught my eye</u>. He came over and asked me to <u>give him a hand</u> carrying his bags to the car. Well, we were just leaving when a shop assistant asked to look in the bags. Full of stolen food! <u>I couldn't believe my eyes!</u> And he <u>nearly died</u> when I told him I'm a police officer and arrested him. I hope <u>he's learnt his lesson</u> ... but I don't suppose he has.

- caught my eye: got my attention
- give him a hand: help him
- I couldn't believe my eyes: I was very, very surprised by what I saw
- nearly died: was very, very surprised/shocked
- he's learnt his lesson: learnt from this experience and so will change his behaviour

Generally, the pronouns and possessive adjectives can change in these idioms. For example, you can say *he caught my eye* or *I caught his eye* or *I learnt my lesson*. We can change the tense of any of the verbs in the idioms.

Exercise 4

1 Fixed
2 Semi-fixed: e.g. *She can't be serious!*
3 Fixed. It is used in the register of formal letters, when you don't know the name or position of the person to whom you are writing.
4 Semi-fixed: e.g. *would he like.*
  Fixed: you cannot say *chips and fish*.
5 Fixed
6 Semi-fixed: e.g. *She'd better ..., They'd better.*

Follow-up activity 1

1 have a headache
2 make a mistake
3 do exercise
4 catch a train

Follow-up activity 2

1 false
2 false
3 false
4 true
5 true

UNIT 5
Exercise 1

1 Lexical: these are all synonyms.
  Grammatical: they are all adjectives (part of speech).
2 Lexical: this is a lexical set with the topic of transport.
  Grammatical: *depart* is the base form of the verb; *bus* and *train* are singular nouns.
3 Lexical: *interested in* is a collocation.
  Grammatical: the grammatical pattern after *interested* is *in* + *-ing* form.
4 Lexical: all the words have the same basic denotation.
  Grammatical: these are different grammatical forms of the verb *go*. *Go* is the base form or the present simple, *going* is the present participle or gerund (*-ing* form), and *went* is the past simple.

Exercise 3

1 <u>In</u> my opinion, this one is <u>the</u> best.
2 Can you advise me <u>on</u> the nicest place to stay?
3 We started <u>at</u> the beginning <u>of</u> September.
4 I'm grateful <u>for</u> the chance to help you.

Exercise 4

1 I really want <u>to try</u> Japanese food.
2 He offered <u>to take</u> me to the airport.
3 I'm interested in <u>learning</u> different languages.
4 She's tired of <u>waiting</u> for them <u>to arrive</u>.

Follow-up activity 1

1 Function words: *I* (pronoun), *'ve* (auxiliary), *been* (used as part of the present perfect continuous).
  Content words: *studying, hard, recently.*
  Grammatical suffixes: *-ing* (in *studying*), *-ly* (in *recently*).
2 Function words: *I* (pronoun), *was* (auxiliary), *to* (a preposition with no lexical meaning – part of the infinitive form), *a* (indefinite article).
  Content words: *asked, give, talk.*
  Grammatical suffix: *-ed* (in *asked*).
3 Function words: *They* (pronoun), *were* (auxiliary), *to* (preposition).
  Content words: *going, school.*
  Grammatical suffix: *-ing* (in *going*).

Follow-up activity 2

1 b   2 d   3 a   4 c

UNIT 6
Exercise 2

looks /lʊks/, *harm* /hɑːm/, *bring* /brɪŋ/, *July*
/dʒuːˈlaɪ/, *these* /ðiːz/. (Note: a small straight line
similar to an apostrophe is used to show the
main stress and is placed immediately before the
stressed syllable; see page 36.)

Notice how some letters are not pronounced
as separate phonemes and so are not written
in the phonemic transcriptions (e.g. the letter
r in *harm*). Also notice that some letters are
pronounced in different ways (e.g. the letter *s* in
looks and *these*).

Exercise 4

For answers to this exercise, see the chart below.

CENTRE

F					
R	iː	ɪ	ʊ	uː	B
O					A
N	e	ə	ɜː	ɔː	C
T					K
	æ	ʌ	ɑː	ɒ	

CENTRE
(adapted from *Sound Foundations* by Adrian
Underhill, Heinemann 1994)

Exercise 5

1 Your lips move back. Your mouth is more
   open for /æ/ than it is for /iː/, in other words,
   your lips should move apart.
2 Your lips make a round shape.
3 You pull your cheeks and lips back but you
   don't open your mouth as wide as you did for
   /æ/.

Exercise 7

1 /b/   2 /f/   3 /ð/   4 /n/   5 /tʃ/   6 /k/   7 /l/

Follow-up activity 1

Monday: 5 phonemes /m/ /ʌ/ /n/ /d/ /eɪ/
student: 8 phonemes /s/ /t/ /j/ /uː/ /d/ /ə/ /n/ /t/
difficult: 8 phonemes /d/ /ɪ/ /f/ /ɪ/ /k/ /ə/ /l/ /t/
flower: 5 phonemes /f/ /l/ /aʊ/ /w/ /ə/

Follow-up activity 2

wh<u>y</u> /aɪ/   say<u>s</u> /z/
pl<u>ease</u> /iː/   gu<u>e</u>ss /e/

Follow-up activity 3

/ˈverɪ/ very   /ˈpiːpəl/ people
/əˈnʌðə/ another   /tʃɪn/ chin

Follow-up activity 4

secretary /ˈsekrətri/   vegetable /ˈvedʒtəbəl/
sure /ʃɔː/   playing /ˈpleɪ(j)ɪŋ/

Follow-up activity 5

/t/ plosive, unvoiced   /s/ fricative, unvoiced
/dʒ/ affricate, voiced   /v/ fricative, voiced
/ŋ/ nasal, voiced

UNIT 7
Exercise 2

1 depen•dency   2 econo•mic   3 biolo•gical
4 tele•vision   5 produc•tion

Suffix	General rule	Example
-y	The syllable third from the end is stressed.	depen•dency
-ic	The syllable second from the end is stressed.	econo•mic
-al	The syllable third from the end is stressed.	biolo•gical
-sion	The syllable second from the end is stressed.	tele•vision
-tion	The syllable second from the end is stressed.	produc•tion

Exercise 3

1 Can you <u>get</u> the <u>children</u>? I'm <u>still</u> at <u>work</u>.
2 <u>What's</u> the <u>best</u> <u>way</u> to <u>get</u> to the <u>station</u>?

Exercise 4

The weak syllables are underlined.
1 I need <u>to</u> <u>or</u>ganise <u>my</u>self.
2 <u>Can</u> I take <u>your</u> photograph?
3 <u>Have</u> <u>you</u> got <u>a</u> notebook?
4 We had dinner <u>and</u> saw <u>a</u> film.
5 <u>Do</u> <u>you</u> like <u>the</u> shirt <u>he</u> bought?

Exercise 6

1 The speaker is probably emphasising that it's a long time or that they are surprised that they've lived here so long.

2 The speaker is emphasising that they do not really believe that the person likes ice cream. The auxiliary is stressed to emphasise the question and express doubt.

3 The speaker is emphasising that they are very pleased. This also sounds polite.

4 The speaker is emphasising their surprise at the price of something.

5 The speaker is emphasising the urgency of the situation/obligation.

Follow-up activity 1

greenhouse (two syllables, noun)

believe (two syllables, verb)

hotel (two syllables, noun. This is one of the exceptions to the two-syllable noun 'rule'.)

suddenly (three-syllables, adverb. The first syllable is often stressed.)

photographic (four syllables, ending in *-ic*, the syllable second from the end is stressed. Alternatively, as a word with four syllables, the stress will be placed somewhere near the middle rather than at the beginning or the end.)

point out (two syllables. The stress is on the second part of this multiword verb.)

good-looking (three syllables. The stress is on the second part of this compound adjective; the first syllable of *looking* is stressed as it is a two-syllable adjective.)

Follow-up activity 2

1 yesterday   2 Paris   3 time

Follow-up activity 3

/ə/

I saw him yesterday

/ə/

She's been to Paris

What time is it? (It is also common to put a secondary stress on *what*.)

Follow-up activity 4

1 Is this your car? (The contrast is the owner of the car.)

2 Do you like coffee/tea/noun? (The contrast is with *like*.)

3 Shall I leave/put it under / next to the table? (The contrast is with the place, i.e. the preposition.) Note: *Where shall I leave this?* is probably wrong because this would mean that the answer has emphatic stress rather than contrastive stress.

UNIT 8
Exercise 1

1 Your voice is more likely to start at a high level.

2 Your voice is more likely to start at a high level. This is often associated with sounding pleased or excited.

Follow-up activity 1

1 High   2 High   3 Low

However, there are different possibilities here, depending on the message the speaker wants to give to the listener.

Follow-up activity 2

1 Fall   2 Fall   3 Rise (but can also fall)

4 Fall   5 Fall

However, there are different possibilities here, depending on the message the speaker wants to give to the listener.

UNIT 9
Exercise 2

• *have* and *not* can move together to make *haven't*. This can happen in speech or in writing. *Have* is a weak form. *Where* and *have* can move together to sound like *where've* /weəv/. This can only happen in speech. We do not write this. *Have* is a weak form.

• *I* and *have* can move together to make *I've*. This can happen in speech or in writing. *I* and *am* can move together to make *I'm*. This can happen in speech or in writing.

• *long* and *have* can move together to make *long've* /ˈlɒŋəv/. This can only happen in speech. We do not write this. *Have* is a weak form.

• *it* and *is* can move together to make *it's*. This can happen in speech or in writing. *It is not* can be contracted to *it's not* /ɪts nɒt/ or *it isn't* /ɪt ɪzənt/. This can happen in speech or in writing.

121

Exercise 3

A: Can you recommend a good hotel in Paris?

B: Um, not really. You should ask Sue. She'd know.

A: OK, thanks. I'll ask her.

B: She's away at the moment, but she'll be back on Tuesday.

Note: the /h/ sound is sometimes dropped or reduced in English. This would mean that the /d/ of *good* would link to the reduced /h/ of *hotel* and the /k/ of *ask* would link to *her*.

Exercise 4

/r/
India and China.

/j/
She asked me to go …

/w/
But I had to ask my boss …

Exercise 5

have to: The voiced sound /v/ can change to /f/ because the following sound /t/ is unvoiced.

this your: The /s/ sound in *this* can change to /ʃ/ to make it easier to continue with the /j/ sound.

could you: /d/ and /j/ can change sound when they occur next to each other; *could* /kʊd/ and *you* /jə/ become /kʊdʒə/. They combine to make the sound /dʒ/. The change that happens to /j/ is an example of assimilation in which the *preceding* sound has an effect.

brown bag: /n/ can become like /m/ because you move your lips together to form the /b/ in *bag*.

Exercise 6

The /d/ in *handbag* can be elided. Note: because the /d/ is elided, the /n/ sound at the end of *han(d)* is now followed by the /b/ in *bag*. This causes an assimilation of /n/ to /m/: /ˈhæmbæg/.

The /t/ in the middle and at the end of *mustn't* can be elided.

The /t/ sounds in these words could be stopped just before they are 'exploded'. Alternatively, they could be glottal sounds.

Follow-up activity 1

I've been studying English for ten months and it's
/aɪv bɪn stʌdjɪŋɪŋglɪʃ   fə temʌnθzənɪts

nearly the end of the course.
nɪəlɪ ðiːjendəv ðə kɔːs/

I've [contraction]
been [weak form]
studying English [consonant–vowel linking]

for [weak form]
ten months [assimilation]
and [weak form]
and it's [consonant–vowel linking]
nearly [no feature of connected speech]
the end [intrusion of /j/]
of [weak form]
end of [consonant–vowel linking]
the [weak form]
course [no feature of connected speech]

Follow-up activity 2

1 You and me: /juːwən miː/
2 Hi, I'm John: /haɪjaɪm/
3 Did you live in town?: /dɪdʒə lɪvɪn/
4 Is she still in bed?: /ɪʃiː/; /ɪmbe(d)/

UNIT 10

Exercise 1

1 b) 2 a) 3 c) 4 d)

In this type of sentence:

- a subject normally comes before a verb
- an indirect object normally comes after a verb
- a direct object normally comes after a verb. The direct object is the thing which is directly acted on by the verb.
- an indirect object often comes before a direct object. It is possible to write *She bought lots of presents for her* where the indirect object follows the direct object. The indirect object is the thing that is affected by the verb but is not directly acted on.

Exercise 3

1 A verb. The past participle of *speak*. We know that *spoken* is a verb partly because it is preceded by a subject pronoun and that it is the past participle of *speak* because it follows the auxiliary *have* (the syntax), and has the letter *o* instead of *ea* in the middle and the letters *-en* at the end (the morphology).

2 An adjective. The past participle of *speak*. We can't tell this just from the morphology, but if we look at the syntax we can see that it is describing the noun *English*.

Follow-up activity 1

1 *told*: verb, transitive, past simple irregular.

me: pronoun, personal, indirect object, first person singular (equivalent to subject pronoun *I*).

problem: noun, singular, countable, direct object.

yesterday: adverb, describing time, can be placed at the beginning or immediately after the indirect object (*me*) or at the end of the sentence.

2 *We*: pronoun, subject, personal, first person plural.
arrived: verb, intransitive, past participle, regular.
the: determiner, definite article (we know which cinema).
earlier: adverb, comparative, change *y* to *i* and add *-er*.

3 *but*: conjunction of contrast, placed between phrases which are contrasted.
completely: adverb of degree, placed before the adjective it describes, add *-ly*.
happy: adjective, placed after verb *be* in a statement.

4 *your*: determiner, possessive adjective.
mine: possessive pronoun, first person singular, used to replace *my book*.
sure: adjective, placed after verb *be* in a statement.

5 *That*: determiner, demonstrative adjective.
boiling: verb, present participle used in the present continuous.
Put: verb, imperative.
it: pronoun, direct object.
down: adverb of direction or place.

Follow-up activity 2

1 *go*: verb or noun
2 *written*: verb (past participle), adjective
3 *myself*: reflexive pronoun
4 *so*: adverb, conjunction
5 *almost*: adverb
6 *like*: preposition (*he's like me*), verb (*I like him*)
7 *drive*: verb, noun
8 *ouch*: exclamation
9 *whereas*: conjunction
10 *when*: adverb, conjunction, pronoun
11 *best*: (superlative) adjective, adverb, noun
12 *all*: determiner, pronoun, adverb

UNIT 11
Exercise 4
oil = noun
old = adjective
of his house = prepositional phrase
friend's = noun with possessive 's'

Exercise 5
1 active
2 useful, useless, usable
3 nervous, nervy
4 rainy
5 amusing, amused
6 written

Exercise 6
1 I've seen many good films, but this one is the best.
2 He's 172 cm tall, and I'm 180, so I'm taller than him.
3 I'm intelligent, John's more intelligent than me but Jo's the most intelligent of all of us.

Follow-up activity 1
1 *a* = determiner (indefinite article); *large* = modifier (adjective); *house* = common noun; *by the sea* = prepositional phrase (*by* = preposition, *the* = determiner (definite article); *sea* = common noun

2 *some* = determiner (quantifier); *lovely* = modifier (adjective); *Spanish* = modifier (adjective); *jewellery* = common noun; *for my birthday* = prepositional phrase (*for* = preposition, *my* = possessive adjective, *birthday* = common, compound, countable noun)

3 *the* = determiner (definite article); *cheap* = modifier (adjective); *green* = modifier (adjective); *one* = pronoun

Follow-up activity 2
1 *lengthy*: noun *length* (nominalisation of *long*) + suffix *-y*. Placed before the noun. Modified by *very*.

2 *exhausted*: ungradable adjective. Modified by intensifier *completely*. Placed after the verb *feeling*.

3 *stormy*: made from the noun *storm* + suffix *-y*. Placed before the noun. *Stormy weather* is a common collocation.

4 *happier*: comparative adjective made from *happy* + *er* (*y* changes to *i*). Placed before the noun.

UNIT 12
Exercise 1
1 *Do* auxiliary; *know* main, state, transitive, reflexive
2 *hurt* main, state, transitive, reflexive
3 *was* auxiliary; *talking* main, action, intransitive
4 *did* auxiliary; *see* main, action, transitive

Exercise 2
1 *depends* + *on* (a dependent preposition) + *the weather* (direct object, noun / noun phrase)
2 *believe* + *in* (a dependent preposition) + *luck* (direct object, noun / noun phrase). *Believe* can also be followed by *in* + *-ing* form (+ noun / noun phrase), e.g. *I believe in helping people.*
3 *remembered* + *to ask* (second verb, the infinitive form) + *Jane* (indirect object, noun / noun phrase). This means that I asked Jane because I remembered to.
4 *remember* + *asking* (second verb, the *-ing* form) + *Jane* (object, noun). This means that I have a memory of something I previously did.

Exercise 3
1 The modal is placed before the main verb in the verb phrase. It is not necessarily placed *directly* before the main verb. It could be separated by an adverb (e.g. *could just see*) or a subject pronoun in a question (e.g. *can you help*).
2 The (main) verb after the modal is the base form (e.g. *can go, might have, might know, can (you) help, can't find*).
3 Questions are formed by putting the modal before the subject (e.g. *can you*). Negatives are formed by adding *not* after the modal (e.g. *cannot/can't*).
4 Modals form their past by using *have* + past participle – the perfect infinitive (e.g. *might have got*). With *must* to express obligation, the past form changes to *had to*.
5 Modals do not change their form to show the person (*he, she, it*, etc.).

Exercise 4
1 b 2 a 3 e 4 c 5 d
Notes:
• Different modals can be used to express the same function. For example, *can* and *could* are used to make requests.

• Different modals can be used to express different 'strengths' of meaning, for example *you must see a doctor.* vs. *you should see a doctor.* Both are giving advice but *must* is often interpreted as stronger advice than *should*.
• Modals sometimes need to change/add to their form or use a different verb in order to express the same meaning in the past. For example, past obligation is expressed by using *had to* and not *must*.

Follow-up activity 1
A: <u>Are</u> [auxiliary *be*] you going out tonight?
B: Yes, with John. <u>Do</u> [auxiliary *do*] you mind?
A: No, of course not. I <u>was</u> [auxiliary *be*] just asking. I'<u>m</u> [main verb *be*] <u>always</u> [adverb of frequency] interested in what you <u>do</u>! [main verb *do*]
B: John'<u>s</u> [auxiliary *have*] <u>been</u> [auxiliary *be*] <u>given</u> [*has been given* = passive voice] some free tickets to a club in the city centre. We'<u>ve</u> [auxiliary *have*] arranged to meet some friends <u>there</u> [adverb of place].
A: It sounds great. I hope you <u>have</u> [main verb *have*] a good time. <u>Can</u> [modal verb] you call me tomorrow?
B: Yes, sure.

Follow-up activity 2
1 Necessity.   3 Advice.
2 Obligation.   4 Deduction.

UNIT 13
Exercise 3
Generally speaking, the perfect aspect relates two times to each other.
1 *I've lived*: Present perfect simple. It connects the past to the present, i.e. the action began in the past and continues now. It is often used with phrases beginning with *for, since* or *how long*.
2 *I'll have been*: Future perfect simple. It connects a point in the present/future to another point in the future. It is often used with phrases beginning with *by*.
3 *Kate's travelled*: Present perfect simple. It connects the past to the present, i.e. the action is at some point in Kate's life, including now. It is used here to express experiences.

4 *She'd been*: Past perfect simple. It relates a point in the past to another point in the past, i.e. visiting Paris happened before she was 15. The second event (being 15) is in the past simple.

Basic form using perfect aspect
Declarative and negative

Name of structure	Subject	Auxiliary have (not)	Main verb: past participle
Present perfect	he	has(n't)	arrived
Future perfect	they	will have	forgotten
Past perfect	I	hadn't	realised

Interrogative

Question word	Auxiliary have	Subject	Main verb: past participle
Where	has	he	gone
	had	she	realised

• The future perfect interrogative structure is: *will* + subject + *have* + past participle.

Exercise 5

1 If <u>I won</u> a million dollars …
2 I wish <u>I was</u> still there now.
3 Every summer, <u>we went</u> to my grandparents' house.
4 <u>We used to drive</u> there.
5 <u>I was walking</u> down the road …
6 <u>The band was playing</u> and <u>lots of people were dancing</u>.
7 At this time yesterday, <u>I was having</u> dinner in Paris!

Exercise 6
Notes for present simple:

• The auxiliary *do/does* is not used in the declarative.
• -*s* is added to the verb in the third person singular (*he, she, it*), e.g. *lives*; -*es* is added to *go* (*goes*) and *do* (*does*).
• If the verb ends in *y*, this changes to *i* when -*es* is added in the third person singular, e.g. *carry – carries*.
• *Be* is irregular (*I am, you are, he is*).

Notes for past simple:

• The auxiliary *did* is not used in the declarative.
• The ending -*ed* (or -*d* when the base form already ends in *e*, e.g. *loved*) is added to regular verbs.
• If the verb ends in *y*, this changes to *i* when -*ed* is added, e.g. *carry – carried*.
• If the verb ends in a single vowel + single consonant, the consonant is doubled and -*ed* is added, e.g. *stop – stopped*.
• There are many irregular forms, e.g. *win – won, go – went, sleep – slept*.

Notes for present and past continuous:

• *Be* agrees with the subject and can often contract in the present continuous: *I am / I'm, I was, you are / you're, you were, he is / he's, he was, we are / we're, we were, they are / they're, they were*.
• The final *e* is dropped when the verb ends in a single consonant + *e*, e.g. *have – having*.
• If the verb ends in a single vowel + single consonant, the consonant is doubled and -*ing* is added, e.g. *stop – stopping*.

Notes for *used to*:

• Declarative: *used to* + base form, e.g. *We used to drive there*.
• Negative/interrogative: *did not* (*didn't*) + *use to*. Notice that the -*d* is dropped because the auxiliary gives the tense.

Exercise 7
Negative

Name of form	Subject	Auxiliary + not	Main verb: base form OR present participle
Present/ Past simple	I	don't/ didn't	want (base form)
Present/ Past continuous	I	am ('m) not / wasn't	working

Answer key for Exercises and Follow-up activities

Interrogative

Name of form	Question word	Auxiliary	Subject	Base form OR present participle
Present/ Past simple	When	do/did	they	go?
Present/ Past continuous	Where	are/were	you	living?

Notes for present and past simple:

- *Do* agrees with the subject in the present simple (*I don't want, he doesn't want, does she want*) and *did* is used for all persons in the past simple (*I didn't want, did they go*).
- Contractions of *do not*: *don't, doesn't, didn't*.

Notes for present and past continuous:

- *Be* agrees with the subject: *I am/was, are/were you, is/was he?*
- Contractions of subject + *be* + *not*: *I'm not, he's not / he isn't, we're not / we aren't, I wasn't, he wasn't, we weren't.*

Exercise 8
Future with *will/shall*: *will/shall* + base form

Example	Meaning/use
1 I'll be forty-three on my next birthday.	To describe a fact or truth happening at a point in the future.
2 <u>Will</u> Manchester United <u>win</u> the match on Saturday, do you think?	To make a prediction about the future.

Form	
Question	Negative
will/shall + subject + base form	subject + *will not (won't)* + base form

Future continuous: *will/shall* + *be* + present participle

Example	Meaning/use
3 This time tomorrow, <u>I'll be driving</u> home, I think.	To predict an event that will happen around a specified time in the future, i.e. it will begin before and continue after the specified time.

4 <u>I'll be seeing</u> the doctor again next Friday; I've got an appointment.	To talk about a planned or scheduled event in the future.

Form	
Question	Negative
will/shall + subject + *be* + *-ing* form	subject + *will not (won't)* + *be* + *-ing* form

Be going to + base form

Example	Meaning/use
5 It's very dark! <u>It's going to rain</u>.	To make a prediction of a future event based on present evidence.
6 I've decided <u>we're going to buy</u> a new car next year.	To talk about a future plan or intention.

Form	
Question	Negative
be (*am, is, are*) + subject + *going to* + base form	subject + *be not* (*I'm not, he's not / he isn't, you're not / you aren't*) + *going to* + base form

Follow-up activity 1

1 past simple interrogative
2 future continuous declarative
3 future with *will* interrogative
4 present simple negative

Follow-up activity 2

1 d   2 b   3 c   4 a

UNIT 14
Exercise 1

There are four clauses:

- John was reading quietly (finite)
- when I walked into the room (finite)
- so I went outside again (finite)
- to make a phone call (non-finite)

Exercise 2

1 As I get older (subordinate), I can't work so hard (main). Complex.
2 John left the house (main) and I left about ten minutes later (main). Compound.
   All the main clauses are finite clauses.

3 The man was very helpful (main) / who spoke to me (subordinate). Complex. The subordinate clause here is in the middle of the main clause. Clauses like this are called embedded clauses. This subordinate clause is a defining relative clause (see page 77).

4 To help my students (subordinate), I correct all homework carefully (main). Complex. The subordinate clause here is a non-finite clause. Non-finite clauses have verbs that do not show tense (e.g. the infinitive form as in this example), present participles (e.g. *Arriving* early, I went straight to my room) and past participles (e.g. *I passed the exam, helped by my teacher*). Subordinate clauses can be finite or non-finite. For example, the subordinate clause in number 3 is finite (who *spoke* to me).

Sometimes, subordinate clauses may seem to stand alone. For example:
A: Is that the man?
B: <u>Who I was telling you about</u>?
A: Yes.
However, they will always be dependent on another clause. In this case, the subordinate clause is dependent on *Is that the man?*. (See 'ellipsis', page 90 in Unit 16.)

Exercise 3

1 Time. *when* = conjunction. Expresses the time at which I walked into the room / what was happening at the time I walked into the room.

2 Result. *so* = conjunction. Expresses the result of John reading quietly, i.e. what happened as a result of John reading quietly.

3 Reason. *because* = conjunction. Expresses the reason why I went outside again.

4 Purpose. No conjunction. *to make* = an infinitive expressing purpose. Expresses the purpose of going outside again.

Exercise 6

1 real, real, all time
2 possible, likely, future
3 impossible, unlikely, present
4 unlikely, unlikely, future
5 impossible, impossible, past

Notes for conditionals:

• Type 0 / zero conditional (e.g. number 1) This type of conditional is used to express general truths, scientific facts and processes.

The use of *if* here does not make the meaning unreal or unlikely and you can also replace *if* with *when*. You can use modal verbs in either or both clauses. You can also use past simple + past simple in this type of conditional. For example, *When I worked hard, I passed exams but when I didn't, I didn't* (a general truth in the past).

• Type 1 / first conditional (e.g. number 2) The present simple is used in the *if* clause to refer to the future here.

• Type 2 / second conditional (e.g. numbers 3 and 4) The past simple is used in the *if* clause to refer to the present/future.

• Type 3 / third conditional (e.g. number 5) The past perfect is used in the *if* clause to refer to the hypothetical or unreal past.

Exercise 7

1 threatening
2 regretting
3 giving excuses
4 giving advice

Exercise 8
Changes to grammatical structures:

Generally speaking, grammatical structures in reported speech are changed to the past, as in the table below.

Direct speech	Reported speech
1 Present simple	Past simple
2 Present perfect simple	Past perfect simple
3 Past continuous	Past perfect continuous
4 *can*	*could*
5 *must*	*had to* (see Unit 13)

Changes using reporting verbs and word order:

1 *She said that*: *that* may be omitted.

2 *He told me that*: with *told*, we need to use an object, e.g. *me, us, them*; *that* may be omitted.

3 *He claimed that*: *claim* expresses the function of the original speaker's words or the reporter's interpretation of these words. *That* can be omitted.

4 The interrogative (a question) word order becomes declarative (a statement): *He asked me if <u>I could come</u>.*

5 *He warned us that*: we use the object pronoun *us*; *that* can be omitted.

Points to note:

- To report a request, use *asked* + object + (*not*) + infinitive form. For example, '*Will you help me?*' – *He asked me to help him.*
- To report an imperative, use *told* (an order) or *asked* (a request) + object + (*not*) + infinitive form. For example, '*Don't talk so loudly.*' – *He told me not to talk so loudly.*
- It is not always necessary to change the grammatical forms when using reported speech. For example, '*I was really happy.*' – *She said that she was really happy.*
- Reporting verbs use different verb patterns, for example *He warned me to finish early* (infinitive), *She insisted I go home* (present simple form).
- When the direct speech is in the past perfect, the reported speech remains in the past perfect.
- Common changes to time and place references, pronouns and possessive adjectives are shown below.

Time		Place	
Direct	Reported	Direct	Reported
now	then	here	there
today	that day	this	that
yesterday	the day before	these	those
this week	that week		
next month	the following month		
tomorrow	the next day		
ago	earlier, previously		
Pronouns		Possessive adjectives	
Direct	Reported	Direct	Reported
I	he, she	my	his, her
we	they	your	my, his, her, their, our
me	him, her	our	their
us	them		
you	I, we, me		

Example:

Direct: '*I must see you tomorrow, in my office, because I can't see you today.*'

Reported: She said that she had to see me in her office the next day because she couldn't see me that day.

Follow-up activity 1

1 My sister told me the good news <u>as soon as I got home</u>.
  Expresses when / the time that I was told the good news.

2 When will you be coming home <u>to see us</u>?
  Expresses the purpose of coming home.

3 The house <u>where I used to live</u> is just round the corner.
  Defines the noun phrase in the main clause. This is a defining relative clause and is embedded.

4 <u>Although I don't really want to</u>, I'm going to have to work late tonight.
  Expresses a contrast with the main clause.

Follow-up activity 2

1 Type 0
2 Type 2
3 Type 1 (a reported Type 1: the original is *Take a break if you want to.*)
4 Type 3

UNIT 15

Exercise 1

Extract 1: text type – recipe

- Organisation: begins with a list of ingredients and how these are prepared (*cheese, finely grated*) – moving to preparation of the dish – moving to cooking instructions – ending with serving suggestions.
- Lexis: food vocabulary; preparation vocabulary (e.g. *cut, brush, grind*); cooking vocabulary (e.g. *bake*).
- Grammatical forms: imperatives (e.g. *Place a narrow …, Repeat with …, bake at 220 °C …*).

Extract 2: text type – letter/email of complaint (Organisation, lexis, etc. will vary a lot depending on the context and audience.)

- Organisation: begins with a statement of the problem/complaint – moving to a more detailed description of the problem/complaint and how it made the writer feel – moving to the action requested by the writer – ending with a set phrase (e.g. *I look forward to hearing from you soon*).
- Lexis: adjectives to describe the situation (e.g. *unacceptable*); (exaggerated) adjectives to describe feelings (e.g. *humiliated*); formulaic phrases (e.g. , *I am writing to complain about, at your earliest convenience*).

- Grammatical forms: past simple to describe the situation (e.g. *I did not have, I left the store*); passives (e.g. *I was informed by …, was refused the item*).

Exercise 2

The answers below are suggestions and there are other possibilities.

1 Probably written. From a letter of application. Formal. The use of *post* shows that it is about a job. The formal lexis (*enquire* and *post*), and the use of a full form (*I would like*) show that it is from a text type that uses formal language.

2 Spoken or written. Probably from a conversation with a friend or an email/text message to a friend. Informal. The same language could be used in speaking or in writing. Emails, and particularly text messages to friends, use language which is very similar or often the same as spoken English. The lexis *Hi* (rather than e.g. *How do you do?*), the contractions, the simple grammar (*how are you doing* vs. *I was wondering how you were*) all show the the text is informal.

3 Written. An academic essay/paper. Formal. The use of lexis associated with academic writing, e.g. *demonstrate, essay* means that this is probably an academic essay/paper. *Demonstrate* is also a formal version of *show*. No contractions are used, which is another sign of formality.

4 Spoken. Announcement at station. Formal. The use of the imperative is typical of public announcement and instructions. The more formal word *proceed* is used instead of *go*. We know this is at a station because of the lexis, i.e. *platform*.

Follow-up activity 1

The answers below are suggestions. Your answers may differ depending on the context you have imagined for the text types.

Text type	Possible feature
A human interest story in a newspaper	• Pictures • Columns • Abbreviations • Contractions • Short paragraphs • Direct speech • Reported speech

Text type	Possible feature
An email to a friend	• Simple grammar • Abbreviations • Contractions • Short paragraphs • Reported speech
Notes taken during a lecture	• Bullet points • Simple grammar • Abbreviations • Contractions
An academic essay	• Complex grammar • Long paragraphs • Reported speech
A shopping list	• A column • Bullet points • Simple grammar, e.g. plurals • Abbreviations

Follow-up activity 2

The answers below are suggestions and there are other possibilities.

Formal	Informal
1 How do you do?	Hi/Hello.
2 We request the pleasure of your company at a dinner to celebrate …	Come to dinner to … / We'd love you to come to dinner … / Would you like to come to dinner?
3 Yours sincerely, …	Lots of love, …
4 Dear Lucy Smith / Ms Smith, …	Hi Lucy, …

UNIT 16
Exercise 2

1 When I arrived at the station
2 the first thing I did was collect my tickets.
3 Next, I went to the platform
4 but my train had been delayed
5 so I went to a café
6 and had a cup of coffee.

Exercise 3

1 *When*: expresses a relationship of time between *I arrived* and *I met Joe and Sue*. It is a subordinating conjunction of time introducing a subordinate clause (see Unit 14). Other examples of subordinating conjunctions are: *as long as, except that, in order to.*

and: relates Joe to Sue and expresses that both are equally important. It is a co-ordinating conjunction used to connect items of equal grammatical importance and show an addition.

but: relates *Sam wasn't there* to *I met* and expresses a relationship of contrast. It is a co-ordinating conjunction used to connect items of equal grammatical importance and show a contrast.

because: relates *Sam wasn't there* to *she was ill* and expresses a reason.

2 *As soon as*: relates *give us your credit card details* to *we can either post or email your tickets* and expresses a relationship of time. It is a subordinating conjunction introducing a subordinate clause (see Unit 14).

either/or: relates two items to each other and expresses a relationship of alternatives.

Exercise 4

2 *they* = John and Sue

3 *It* = a long journey

4 *Here* = the website address for times: www.traintimes.org

5 *These* = seats (refers to something that is not in the text itself. We can guess that the speaker means 'seats' from the context and the utterance is probably accompanied by a gesture such as pointing to the seats).

6 *this* = a physical direction (the sign probably has an arrow pointing in the direction that *this* refers to).

Exercise 5

2 *they* = an anaphoric reference, a pronoun.

4 *Here* = a cataphoric reference, an adverb.

6 *this* = an exophoric reference, a determiner.

Exercise 6

1 *which* and *It* = (We saw) *the sun coming up*. (anaphoric references)

2 *that* = (I once) *went to Italy on holiday*. (anaphoric reference)

3 *This* = *Don't touch the red or the black wires*. (cataphoric reference)

4 *the following* = *sign in to your account again; reload this software; call our help desk*. (cataphoric reference)

5 *This is why* = *She's very sociable and generous*. (anaphoric reference)

Follow-up activity 1

1 A: Do you like coffee and tea? B: Yes, I do. Substitution of *do* (for *like*); ellipsis of *coffee and tea*.

2 We know Clare well. You'll like her. Substitution of *her* (for *Clare*)

3 John likes football and tennis but he doesn't play either/them well. Substitution of *he* (for *John*) and *either/them* (for *football and tennis*)

4 I need a new pen and Sue does too. Substitution of *does* (for *needs*); ellipsis of *a new pen*.

Follow-up activity 2
Check-in

<u>This</u> [substitution and anaphoric reference to the title *Check-in*] is an important part of <u>your</u> [cataphoric reference to *you*] airport experience. <u>Firstly</u> [to order the reasons], <u>because</u> [to show reason] <u>you</u> [anaphoric reference to *your*] will meet <u>our</u> [exophoric reference] friendly staff <u>who</u> [anaphoric reference to *staff*] can provide information about your flight, <u>and</u> [shows next clause has equal importance] <u>secondly</u> [to order the reasons] because you will be able to choose the seat you want. <u>For these reasons</u> [anaphoric reference to previous clause, *these* to emphasise the clause and show writer is referring to something nearby in the text] you should arrive early at your terminal. <u>After</u> [to show order of procedure] checking in, you should go to passport control.

Lexical chain: *check-in, airport, flight, seat, terminal, passport control*.

Parallelism: use of *should* + base form.

UNIT 17
Exercise 2
line 1

So helps start the conversation. It also tells the listener that A is going to speak. *what do you think?* helps start the conversation and tells the listener that it is their turn to speak. This is done by asking a general question and giving the listener something to talk about.

line 2

or the … tells the listener that it is their turn to speak. This is done by giving a conjunction that needs a noun but pausing and not providing the noun, inviting A to provide the noun and continue the conversation.

line 3

think it's OK? tells the listener that it is their turn to speak. This is done by giving the listener something to talk about.

line 6

Yeah lets the speaker know that B is listening. It makes B sound interested.

Follow-up activity 1

1 d   2 c   3 a   4 b

Follow-up activity 2

Sue: Hi. <u>How's it going?</u> [opening the conversation, offering a turn to John – turn-taking]

Sue: <u>Oh dear</u> … [back-channelling, showing sympathy]

Sue: <u>Poor you</u> [back-channelling, showing sympathy]

Sue: <u>Er</u> [hesitating] … <u>well,</u> [introducing a solution]

John: Good … <u>I mean</u> [introducing a reformulation]

Sue: <u>Anyway</u> [changing the topic], <u>sorry, but I really need to go.</u> [closing the conversation]

UNIT 18

Exercise 1

The meanings of all the words and sentences from the table change because of the context. The speaker's/writer's intended meaning is more than the semantic meaning of these words and sentences.

1 I'm offering to open the window to make us cooler. / I'm suggesting we open the window to make us cooler.

2 I'm uncomfortably warm. / I'd like you to help me get cooler. / I'd like you to turn the air-con up.

3 I'm annoyed that you haven't booked the flight. / You should have booked the flight. / I want you to book the flight as soon as possible.

4 Can I speak to your brother on the phone, now? / I want you to fetch your brother.

5 No smoking. / Please don't smoke. / You aren't allowed to smoke.

6 No talking. / You aren't allowed to talk. / Talking is forbidden.

Exercise 2

Dialogue 1 Pragmatic meaning

A: Are you a chicken man? = Do you like chicken?

Function: Asking about preference

Context: Two people planning what to eat for dinner.

Comment: The meaning here would be very strange to someone who only understood the semantic meaning.

Dialogue 2 Pragmatic meaning

A: Do you know what the time is? = I'm angry/irritated that you're late.

Function: Complaining, expressing irritation

Context: Two people who know each other quite well. A might look at his/her watch so that it is obvious he/she is not asking for the time. It is not acceptable to arrive home late and A is angry.

Exercise 3

Note: not all the alternatives given below can be used in extracts 1 and 2 because their register may be different.

Extract 1

OK

• Shows the listener you are going to say something

• Starts the conversation
  Alternatives: *now, well*

in fact

• Indicates a fact (in your opinion)

• Emphasises what you are saying
  Alternatives: *actually*

I mean

• Introduces a clarification or reformulation

• Gets the listener's attention
  Alternatives: *you know, in other words, or rather*

So

• Introduces a summary or clarification of previous language

• Signals that the speaker is checking their understanding
  Alternatives: *then, just to clarify, you mean*

Answer key for Exercises and Follow-up activities

Extract 2

Frankly

- Introduces an honest opinion or thought (often a strong and/or critical opinion)
  Alternatives: *to be honest, honestly, to tell you the truth*

amazingly

- Introduces something surprising or strange
  Alternatives: *strangely, surprisingly, astonishingly*

Apparently

- Introduces something you were told by others, which may or may not be true
  Alternatives: *seemingly, it would appear that*

actually

- Introduces a fact (in your opinion)
  Alternatives: *in fact, in truth, truthfully*

Anyway

- Introduces a result or conclusion
- Shows you have stopped giving details and are moving to the next point
- Changes the topic direction
  Alternatives: *so, at the end of the day*

obviously

- Indicates something that is clear and obvious (in your opinion)
  Alternatives: *clearly, of course*

By the way

- Changes the discourse to a new topic
  Alternatives: *incidentally, anyway*

Unfortunately

- Introduces something disappointing or bad
  Alternatives: *sadly, disappointingly, I'm afraid*

Follow-up activity 1

1 d)   2 c)   3 b)   4 a)

Follow-up activity 2

amazingly: expresses something very surprising; it is the writer's attitude.
of course: expresses something that is clear to everyone.
obviously: expresses something that is clear to everyone.
in fact: expresses something that is true; here it is the writer's opinion.
Sadly: expresses something that is sad or unlucky; it is the writer's attitude.

Answer key for TKT: KAL practice tasks

UNIT

1	1 B	2 C	3 A	4 G	5 D	6 F		
2	1 D	2 C	3 A	4 C	5 B	6 A	7 C	
3	1 B	2 A	3 F	4 D	5 E	6 C		
4	1 B	2 C	3 B	4 A	5 C	6 B		
5	1 F	2 B	3 E	4 D	5 C	6 A		
6	1 C	2 B	3 A	4 B	5 A	6 C		
7	1 D	2 E	3 F	4 G	5 B	6 A		
8	1 A	2 B						
9	1 D	2 C	3 B	4 A	5 C	6 B	7 D	
10	1 B	2 B	3 A	4 B	5 A	6 C		
11	1 B	2 C	3 D	4 E	5 G	6 A		
12	1 A	2 C	3 B	4 C	5 B			
13	1 G	2 C	3 D	4 A	5 B	6 F	7 H	
14	1 D	2 A	3 B	4 F	5 G	6 E		
15	1 A	2 B	3 A	4 C	5 B	6 C		
16	1 A	2 A	3 B	4 C	5 C	6 B		
17	1 B	2 B	3 A	4 C	5 A			
18	1 A	2 B	3 A	4 C	5 B			

Answer key for TKT: KAL practice test

1 C	2 G	3 H	4 D	5 A	6 F	7 B	8 I	
9 F	10 B	11 A	12 D	13 E				
14 C	15 B	16 C	17 B	18 A	19 B	20 B		
21 D	22 A	23 D	24 C	25 B	26 C	27 D	28 C	29 B
30 B	31 A	32 C	33 B	34 A	35 C			
36 B	37 B	38 C	39 A	40 C	41 C	42 C	43 B	44 B
45 C	46 A	47 B	48 A	49 B	50 B			
51 G	52 E	53 F	54 A	55 B	56 I	57 C	58 H	
59 C	60 A	61 B	62 A	63 C	64 B	65 A		
66 C	67 B	68 B	69 A	70 A	71 A	72 B	73 A	74 B
75 B	76 A	77 C	78 C	79 B	80 A			

Alphabetical list of glossary terms

Terms in *italic* are in the *TKT Glossary* published by Cambridge ESOL. Terms that are not in italic are also in the TKT Glossary but are exclusive to the TKT: KAL. The page references show where the terms are defined or exemplified. Where a term is discussed in more detail, the page reference is given in **bold**.

Alphabetical list of glossary terms

Unit-by-unit list of glossary terms

Terms in *italic* appear in the *TKT Glossary* published by Cambridge ESOL. Terms that are not in italic also appear in the *TKT Glossary* but are exclusive to the TKT: KAL. Any of the terms, those in italic and those not (and those in the *TKT Glossary* not included here) may appear in the TKT: KAL.

Unit 1
adverb
collocation
colloquial
connotation
context
delexicalised
denotation
figurative (meaning)
formal (language)
function
idiom
informal (language)
lexis
literal meaning
multiword verb
particle
preposition
register
style

Unit 2
antonym
connotation
context
false friend
formal (language)
homonym
homophone
hyponym
informal (language)
lexical set
register
superordinate
synonym
topic
varieties of English

Unit 3
abbreviation
acronym
adjective
adverb
affix
affixation
apostrophe
base word
compound
contraction
form
initialism
morpheme
noun
part of speech
particle
past participle
prefix
preposition
present participle
register
root word
suffix
verb
word family

Unit 4
adverb
chunk
collocate
collocation
context
discourse
figurative (meaning)
idiom
idiomatic
informal (language)
literal (meaning)
pronoun

register
tense
verb

Unit 5
adjective
adverb
aspect
auxiliary verb
collocation
comparative adjective
content word
dependent preposition
feature
form
function word
gerund
infinitive form
-ing form
lexis
morpheme
noun
object
part of speech
particle
past participle
past simple tense
phrasal verb
present participle
present perfect simple
present simple tense
subject
suffix
superlative adjective
verb

Unit 6
affricate
alveolar ridge
bilabial

Unit-by-unit list of glossary terms

consonant
consonant cluster
diphthong
fricative
labio-dental
minimal pair
nasal
palate
phoneme
phonemic chart
phonemic symbol
phonemic transcription
plosive
unvoiced
variety of English
velar
voiced
vowel

Unit 7

adjective
adverb
compound noun
content word
contrastive stress
emphatic
function word
main stress
noun
phonemic transcription
primary stress
rhythm
schwa
secondary stress
sentence stress
suffix
syllable
verb
vowel
weak form
word class
word stress

Unit 8

contrastive (stress)
discourse
emphatic
imperative

intonation
primary stress
question tag
secondary (stress)
wh- question

Unit 9

assimilation
auxiliary verb
connected speech
consonant
contraction
elision
emphasise
emphatic
formal (language)
glottal (stop)
infinitive form
informal (language)
intrusion
intrusive
linking
past simple
phonemic transcription
register
strong form
style
syllable
unvoiced sound
voiced sound
vowel
weak form
word boundary

Unit 10

adjective
adverb
affixation
clause
conjunction
determiner
form
informal
morpheme
noun
noun phrase
object
part of speech

phrase
prefix
preposition
pronoun
subject
suffix
syntax
verb
word class

Unit 11

abstract (noun)
adjective
adverb
affixation
article
determiner
collective noun
common noun
comparative adjective
complex (clause)
compound
compound noun
concrete (noun)
countable noun
demonstrative adjective
gerund
gradable
intensifier
modifier
noun
noun phrase
part of speech
past participle
phrase
possessive adjective
possessive 's'
present participle
proper noun
qualify
quantifier
relative clause
suffix
superlative adjective
uncountable noun
ungradable
verb
verb phrase

Unit 12

active voice
adjective
adverb
adverbial
auxiliary verb
causative passive
clause
complement
context
dependent preposition
dynamic verb
function
hypothetical
infinitive form
-ing form
intransitive verb
modal verb
multiword verb
noun phrase
object
passive voice
past participle
past simple
present simple tense
reflexive pronoun
semi-modal verb
stative (state) verb
subject
tense
transitive verb
verb
verb pattern
verb phrase
verbs of perception

Unit 13

aspect
auxiliary verb
complex
context
declarative form
form
future form
future with going to
grammatical structure
-ing form

interrogative
past continuous/progressive
past participle
past perfect simple
present continuous/progressive
present participle
present simple
subject
tense
used to
verb
wh- word

Unit 14

auxiliary verb
clause
conditional
conjunction
connector
co-ordinating conjunction
declarative
direct speech
finite verb
form
function
grammatical structure
hypothetical
imperative
indirect object
infinitive form
infinitive of purpose
interrogative
main clause
mixed conditional
modal verb
non-finite verb
noun phrase
object
past continuous/progressive
past perfect
past simple
person
present continuous/progressive
present perfect
present simple
pronoun
reduced relative clause

regular verb
relative clause
relative pronoun
reported speech
reporting verb
subject
subordinate clause
subordinating conjunction
Type 1 or first conditional
Type 2 or second conditional
Type 3 or third conditional
verb phrase

Unit 15

complex
context
contraction
dialogue
finite verb
form
formal (language)
grammatical structure
informal (language)
layout
main clause
past simple
present continuous/progressive
present perfect continuous
present perfect simple
register
style
subject
subordinate clause
text type
utterance

Unit 16

adverb
adverbial
anaphoric reference
base form
cataphoric reference
coherence
coherent
cohesion
cohesive
cohesive device
comparative adjective

Unit-by-unit list of glossary terms

conjunction
determiner
ellipsis
exophoric reference
lexical chain
lexical set
lexis
parallelism
past continuous/progressive
pronoun
register
rhythm
substitution
suffix
text type
topic
word family

Unit 17
back-channelling
cohesive device
conjunction
context
dialogue
discourse
discourse marker
ellipsis
formal (language)
hesitation
informal (language)
intonation
lexis
paraphrase
reformulation
register
repair strategy
substitution
summarise
text type
turn-taking
utterance

Unit 18
adverb
clause
context
discourse marker
formal (language)
function
informal (language)
intonation
literal meaning
pragmatic meaning
preposition
rhetorical question
semantic meaning
topic
utterance